Paul Manship: Changing Taste in America

D1568538

Paul Manship

Changing Taste in America

19 May to 18 August 1985
Minnesota Museum of Art
Landmark Center, Saint Paul

This project is supported by generous grants from the National Endowment for the Humanities, National Endowment for the Arts, Federal agencies; the Minnesota Humanities Commission; and West Publishing Company, Saint Paul.

Additional support for the project has been provided by the Mary Livingston Griggs and Mary Griggs Burke Foundation, Saint Paul; and by the late Lila Acheson Wallace, New York. The Saint Paul presentation of the exhibition has been made possible by the generous assistance of Saint Paul Ramsey United Arts Council, Institute of Museum Services, Minnesota State Arts Board, Ramsey County Commissioners, The United Arts Fund, and Dayton Hudson Foundation: B. Dalton Booksellers, Daytons, and Target Stores.

(cover)
44. *Flight of Night,* 1916
gilded bronze
26¼ x 31 x 8
Collection Minnesota Museum of Art,
Gift of Mrs. Arthur H. Savage
58.02.03

(frontispiece)
36. *Fame,* 1926
pink Georgia marble
26 x 28 x 4½
66.14.101

NOTE TO THE CATALOGUE

Unless otherwise indicated, all works illustrated in the catalogue are in the collection of Minnesota Museum of Art, Bequest of the Estate of Paul Howard Manship.

Dimensions for drawings and sculpture are given in inches; height precedes width precedes depth. Measurements include base size.

Catalogue entries were prepared by: Jean F. Hunter (J.F.H.), Gloria Kittleson (G.K.), Leanne Klein (L.A.K.) and Susan Levy (S.L.).

Standard sources were used in the preparation of entries, unless otherwise noted. Thomas Bulfinch, *Bulfinch's Mythology* (New York: Avenel Books, 1982), and J.E. Zimmerman *Dictionary of Classical Greek Mythology,* (New York: Harper & Row, 1964), were consulted for the mythological references.

All works in the exhibition are illustrated in the catalogue, and numbered with their respective entries (with the exception of those works listed on page 157). Works referred to in the context of an essay or entry are followed by this number, given in parentheses.

Murtha numbers, e.g. (Murtha 27), refer to the catalogue entry numbers in the monograph *Paul Manship* by Edwin Murtha, (New York: The Macmillan Company, 1957), the *catalogue raisonné* of Manship's work.

Acknowledgments

Many individuals and organizations have offered assistance and expertise in the development of the exhibition and preparation of its catalogue. I am deeply grateful to Dr. Harry Rand, Curator, Painting and Sculpture, National Museum of American Art, Smithsonian Institution, who acted as adviser and consultant for the Manship project, and who wrote the lead essay for the catalogue. Special thanks are due David H. Katzive, Head of Museum Television Production Services of Lexington, Massachusetts, who wrote and directed the videotape; and to the following consultants who participated in the videotape: Gregory B. Free, architectural historian, Old Texas Properties, who supervised the restoration of the Manship house in Jackson, Mississippi; Susan Rather, Research Fellow, Smithsonian Institution, Ph.D. candidate, University of Delaware, and Dr. William M. Stott, Professor of American Studies and English, Director, American Studies Programs, The University of Texas at Austin.

Minnesota Museum of Art gratefully acknowledges Dr. Charles C. Eldredge, Director and Dr. Elizabeth Broun, Assistant Director and Chief Curator, National Museum of American Art, for arranging the generous loan of twenty-two works from its collection. Their collaboration has made it possible for us to enlarge the scope of the exhibition.

We are especially grateful to the following members of the Manship family: John Manship, Mrs. Paul K. Manship, Mrs. O.N. Klatt, William Manship, and other relatives for their helpful advice and for sharing Manship letters and papers, as well as lending works for the Saint Paul showing.

Nearly the entire museum staff was involved. Their readiness to lend support was invaluable. I would like to express my appreciation to Leanne Klein, Associate Curator for Collections Management, for overseeing loans, conservation and registration; Leanne, together with Patricia Heikenen, offered expert editorial assistance. Jean Hunter, Assistant Curator for Research, Leanne Klein and Susan Levy, Research Assistant, exhibited great dedication and enthusiasm, contributed most of the catalogue entries and developed files that will be of value for future scholarly research. Susan, additionally, prepared the bibliography. Thanks are due Joanna Baymiller for overseeing the videotape production and for administering, with Janet Bisbee, the half-dozen grants which fund the project, and to my predecessor, Thomas Holman, whose early work helped ensure these funds; to Karen Mueller who organized a symposium and a series of public programs related to the exhibition, and to consultant Jack El-Hai for a film series. Many thanks are extended to James Ristine for his creative design of the exhibition, to Stafford Taylor, Timothy White and David Madzo, who assisted with the installation; to Julie Schreifels for designing the exhibition graphics; and to James J. Kamm and the Support Program staff. Lastly, I wish to express special thanks to Jim Czarniecki for his encouragement and support throughout the entire project.

Gloria Kittleson
Curator of Collections

Lenders to the Exhibition

The Art Institute of Chicago*

Augsburg College Permanent Collection

Bradley Bonse and
Florence Manship Bonse*

Michael Birdsall and Roger Haase

Corcoran Gallery of Art
Washington, D.C.

Cowan Pottery Museum
Rocky River, Ohio

American Museum —
Hayden Planetarium*

Mr. and Mrs. O.N. Klatt*

Lachaise Foundation, Courtesy Robert
Schoelkopf Gallery, Ltd.

The Marion Koogler McNay Art Museum
San Antonio, Texas

Mr. and Mrs. John Manship

Mrs. Paul K. Manship*

The Minneapolis Institute of Arts

Montclair Art Museum
Montclair, New Jersey

National Museum of American Art
Smithsonian Institution

Solon Borglum Sculpture Project

Mr. and Mrs. Thomond R. O'Brien

Mr. and Mrs. Gerald P. Peters

Smith College Museum of Art
Northampton, Massachusetts

*Saint Paul showing only

Exhibition Tour

Hudson River Museum
Yonkers, New York
10 November 1985 - 5 January 1986

Norton Gallery & School of Art,
West Palm Beach, Florida
1 February - 15 March 1986

Dayton Art Institute
Dayton, Ohio
8 November 1986 - 4 January 1987

Lakeview Museum of Arts and Sciences
Peoria, Illinois
8 February - 23 March 1987

Colorado Springs Fine Arts Center
Colorado Springs, Colorado
16 August - 18 October 1987

Contents

Paul Manship

Phila 1906-7 by himself - aged 23 yrs.

Preface

Paul Manship: Changing Taste in America celebrates the centennial of the artist's birth in Saint Paul, Minnesota. For the first time, a generous selection of works, including twenty-two sculptors and drawings from the Smithsonian Institution's National Museum of American Art, will be shown with drawings, medals and sculpture from the collection of Minnesota Museum of Art. The artist's bequest in 1966 provided for equal division of his personal collection between the two museums. Today, MMA's Manship holdings (more than 350 objects) comprise the largest body of work by a single artist in the Museum's collections.

Furthering the Museum's mission "to collect, preserve, exhibit and interpret American and non-Western art...and to provide art instruction," this project emphasizes the focus of that mission — American art from the late nineteenth to mid-twentieth centuries. It also addresses three specific objectives:
- relating MMA-organized exhibitions more closely to museum collections;
- increasing the Museum's emphasis on the art and art history of the region;
- improving MMA's curatorial services to the field.

As such, *Paul Manship: Changing Taste in America* joins other recent efforts of the Museum (*American Drawing, 1927-1977, Prairie School Architecture, Melanesian Images, American Style, African Art: Power, Wisdom and Passages,* and the series of *Discovery Gallery* and *Gallery 208* exhibitions featuring new artists and new media in the region) in advancing its role in the Twin Cities cultural community, as well as in the museum community regionally and nationally. Commitments such as these are indicative of the vision and support sustained by the Museum's Board of Trustees and the imagination and skill displayed by the Museum's staff.

The Museum's Manship centennial coincides with a nation-wide revival of interest in the artist's work, the restoration and reinstallation of several of his public monuments, and a campaign to encourage the U.S. Postal Service to mark the centennial with a 1985 secular Christmas stamp featuring his best known work, *Prometheus* (fitting tribute for an artist born on Christmas Eve!)

Proclamations honoring International Museum Day and Paul Manship's

2. *Ram's Head from Athens Museum*, 1912
pencil on paper
6 x 8¼
81.01.01
Collection Minnesota Museum of Art
Gift of Dr. and Mrs. John E. Larkin, Jr.

This drawing is of a ram's head sculpted from a block of stone. Manship has dated the drawing "April 14, 1912, Athens National Museum," indicating it was done while visiting Greece during his student days at the American Academy in Rome. This is probably a portion of a pediment on view in the museum at the time of Manship's visit.

Manship had great respect for the principles of Greek architecture, particularly its interrelationship with sculpture.
J.F.H.

Gaston Lachaise (1882–1935)
3. *Small Draped Woman*, 1910
bronze
11 high
Lachaise Foundation
Courtesy Robert Schoelkopf Gallery, Ltd.

This figure of a woman is from a group of small-scaled works of the female form completed by Lachaise between 1910–1915. *Small Draped Woman* shows the influence of Rodin with its impressionistic, modeled surfaces. Lachaise joined Manship shortly after the Armory Show of 1913 and worked as a full-time assistant for seven years, overseeing the other studio assistants. Lachaise was highly regarded by Manship who appreciated his solid grounding in the

legacy have been issued for 18 May 1985, by the Honorable Rudy Perpich, Governor of Minnesota. The artist's native city similarly has chosen to proclaim its appreciation; this honor is bestowed by the Honorable George Latimer, Mayor of Saint Paul.

The Museum wishes to thank Rick Beard, Hudson River Museum, Bruce Weber and Dick Madigan of the Norton Gallery & School of Art, Bruce H. Evans and Kent Sobotik, the Dayton Art Institute, and John Buchanan, the Lakeview Museum of the Arts and Sciences, for their participation in the exhibition tour. Their early commitment to the project ensured realization at a scope that otherwise would not have been attainable.

The entire Manship project, this publication, the exhibition, broadcast-quality videotape and comprehensive interpretive program, would not have been possible without the financial support of several contributors. MMA is especially grateful for major support from the National Endowment for the Humanities and the National Endowment for the Arts, Federal agencies; the Minnesota Humanities Commission; and West Publishing Company, Saint Paul.

Additional funding for the project has been provided by the Mary Livingston Griggs and Mary Griggs Burke Foundation, Saint Paul; and by the late Lila Acheson Wallace, New York. The Saint Paul installation of the exhibition has been made possible through the generous

French Tradition, as well as his sensitive skill as a carver. Lachaise did the actual work on a number of Manship's commissions, such as the inscribed bas reliefs for the New York Telephone and Telegraph Company building. Both artists were fascinated with the female form and animal subjects — Lachaise with his peacocks and dolphins, Manship with his array of animals and birds that populate several zoo gateways; both artists had specific approaches to form, each respecting the other's work.

Lachaise's mature works, dating from around 1927, have a quality of largesse and abundance. His smooth, organic forms, with their weightless, rhythmic grace suggest a debt to Manship.
G.K.

assistance of the Saint Paul/Ramsey United Arts Council. To each of these patrons the Museum is most grateful.

The scope and texture of the exhibition would have been impossible without the generosity and understanding of the lenders to the project. On behalf of the Board of Trustees, I wish to thank them for their participation.

The initial impetus for the exhibition can be traced back further than the two years of involvement by most of us. In 1965, at Saint Paulite Ben Storey, Sr.'s urging, and with journalist Gareth Hiebert's (Oliver Towne's) public encouragement, Laurene Tibbetts, then Director of the Minnesota Museum Art School, visited Paul Manship at his Gloucester, Massachesetts, studio shortly before his death. Her visit convinced the artist that the Museum would be a suitable place to preserve a major portion of works still in his possession. The bequest led to a 1972 exhibition of a selection of works from the collection and, ultimately, to the planning of this centennial effort.

The Museum's gratitude is due to Curator of Collections Gloria Kittleson, who served as exhibition curator, publications editor and project director for all aspects of *Paul Manship: Changing Taste in America*. I add my personal thanks for an exemplary accomplishment. The project has demonstrated MMA's ability to achieve results of a scope and quality usually found among institutions several times its size.

Lastly, Paul Manship himself must be thanked, not only for the objects we view here, but for furnishing insight into our role as viewer: "I have always contended that art must be appreciated by the people," Manship said, "and when art becomes too much of a game between the artist and his small group of sympathizers — or big, as the case may be — it isn't complete."

It is in this role that the Museum acts as catalyst — making art complete — and, in the case of Paul H. Manship, encouraging a greater appreciation within the community that nurtured his artistic growth.

M.J. Czarniecki III
Director

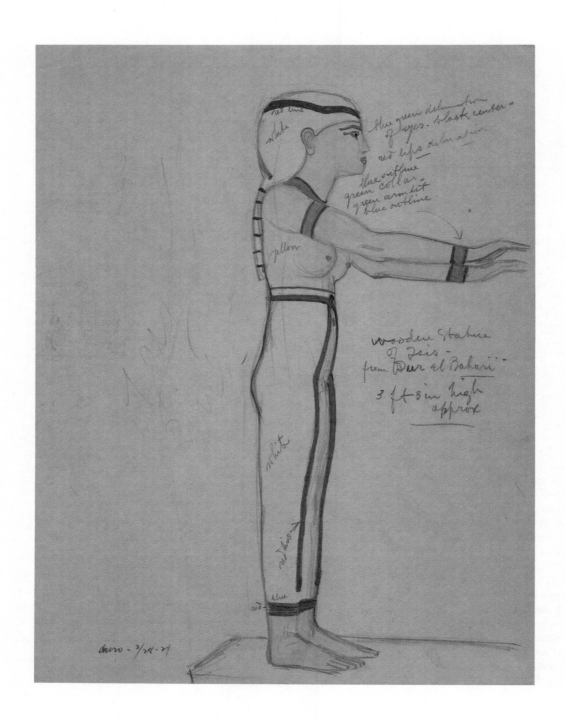

Introduction

Manship considered Egyptian drawings of high excellence and in his treatise on sculpture stated they are "characterized by freedom of spirit, good humour and delight of the artisan in his craft."*

That Manship would have chosen a rare wooden sculpture from which to draw the figure Isis reflects the artist's sensibility to the volumetric as well as the relief conventions of Egyptian art. It is well known that the earlier archaic Egyptian conventions influenced Greek art, as seen in the figure Isis, with her immobile pose. A protectress of the dead, she is seen here with arms upraised in a gesture of blessing.

Scenes from daily life were painted in registers or bands on the walls in tombs of noblemen and pharoahs, ensuring the deceased that the presence of their worldly associations would be with them in the hereafter. Manship has captured the schematic rhythm of the Egyptian artist in the *Egyptian Fresco* (5) watercolor of boatmen, where the typical view of the body is presented from an angle showing its best proportions; the diagonal leg pose, with full chest toward the viewer and full frontal representation of the eye, according to Egyptian canons, reflected the highest powers of the individual.

*Encyclopaedia Brittannica, 1940, 14th Edition, 198.
G.K.

The exhibition *Paul Manship: Changing Taste in America* commemorates the 100th birthday of a native Saint Paul sculptor, at a time when interest in his work is on the ascendant. Several factors emphasize this revival on a nationwide scale. A number of exhibitions this year include Manship's work: the National Museum of American Art is presenting *Zoo to Art: Animal Subjects by American Sculptors;* the Parrish Art Museum, Southampton, New York, features *Fauns and Fountains: American Garden Statuary, 1890-1930;* the Sterling and Francine Clark Institute, Williamstown, Massachusetts, focuses on studies and sketches by American sculptors; the Cornish, New Hampshire, Historic Site highlights the work of Saint-Gaudens and his circle; the Meadows Museum of Art and Centenary College, Shreveport, Louisiana, devotes an exhibition to classical and mythological themes. Another element in this current revival is the recent reinstallation of two Manship sculptures, a man and a woman representing humanity, at a location near their original sites, flanking the recently regilded *Prometheus Fountain* figure in Rockefeller Center. The heightened interest in Art Deco is also a factor — Manship's style matured during the 1920s and 1930s and his work reflected the elegant stylizations associated with that movement.

Works of art form the bases for later assessment of an artist's historical and aesthetic importance. With attention and prominence once again being given to Manship after a period when his work was perceived by some to have fallen out of favor, there is reason to consider it again — to stand back, to view it from all sides, to reassess. To present an exhibition that examines changing taste — both public and critical — is a fitting approach for a museum. It seems logical in Manship's case, since public acceptance of his work was never really lacking, while the critics' reaction, favorable at first, began to wane following World War II. At the 1939 New York World's Fair, Manship's popularity was at its zenith. With the advent of World War II, commencing soon after the fair opened, Manship's work was no longer particularly popular with the critics, and Abstract Expressionism monopolized their attention. The change was a gradual one, as is often the case with public taste; Manship was always embraced by his patrons and the public alike. The shift in critical reaction was more sudden; it rejected Manship's academic art with its emphasis on

6. *Sketch of the Peplos Kore,* 1924
pencil on paper
13⅝ x 10⅛
66.14.155

In his article on sculpture for the
Encyclopaedia Brittannica, Manship referred
to these figures as the "Smiling Maidens"
of the Athenian Acropolis.* Manship drew
this Kore figure on a visit to the Acropolis
Museum, while teaching at the American
Academy in Rome, some twelve years
following his student days there. Manship
shows fidelity in his representation of the
Kore, 530-525 B.C., who was considered
a votive figure and originally placed
outside one of the temples. Her archaic
smile animates her features without
disturbing her face. The elaborate
decorative hairdo contrasts with her
diaphanous dress scarcely suggesting the
body beneath.
    Manship was quick to assimilate the
robust beauty and charm of archaic Greek
korai figures, which he expressed in a
similar kore figure for the Harold
McCormick gardens, Lake Forest, Illinois.
One of eight terminal figures marking
garden avenues, *Calypso* is frontal, the
upper portion of her body more
naturalistic while the lower part is severely
architectural. Her gestures are mannered
and deliberate as she carefully holds up the
hem of her dress in one hand and a flower
in the other.
Encyclopaedia Brittannica, 1940, 14th
edition, 199.
G.K.

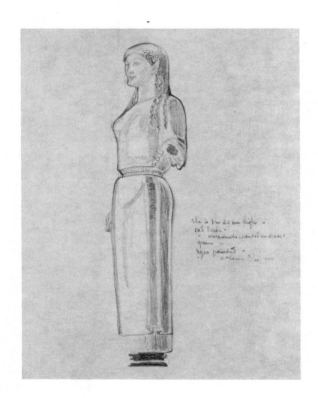

Fig. 1
Calypso, 1914
marble
Commissioned for Harold McCormick
Lake Forest, Illinois (present location
unknown)
Murtha 61

5. *Egyptian Fresco*, n.d.
watercolor on paper
9 x 12½
Collection Mr. and Mrs. Bruce Carlson

craftsmanship and its explicit representational content. His work was
regarded as surface — it reflected the world, but it did not probė it.
Except for isolated larger commissions in the 1950s and 1960s, most of
his late work was dismissed as outmoded. In the 1980s, however, the
legacy of Manship's work as a whole once again commands center stage.
The artist who continued the tradition of outdoor public sculpture that
thrived between the Civil War and World War I, and came to prominence
between the two great wars, deserves another look. This exhibition,
accompanying videotape and catalogue, attempt to address the Manship
legacy. His fine craftsmanship is again appreciated, and his optimistic
themes, akin to Matisse's themes of pleasure and "joy in living," suit our
present taste.

The Manship project attempts, as well, to address the issue of
changing taste in America and chart the shifting national moods that
caused it. The exhibition and catalogue focus on a wide range of themes
within Manship's work: archaism, classicism, mythology, streamlining,
garden sculpture, animal themes, medals, portraits and war and peace
memorials. The essays discuss various apsects of Manship's work: Dr.
Harry Rand, National Museum of American Art, in the lead essay, places
Manship in a larger art historical context, focuses on the European scene
during the first part of the twentieth century, and acknowledges the
artist's debt to the East. His analysis of Manship's relationship to the Art
Deco movement is particularly insightful. Dr. Frederick D. Leach,
Hamline University, who wrote the definitive essay in the Museum's 1972
catalogue, *Paul Howard Manship: An Intimate View,* looks at Manship anew
from an art critic's viewpoint and examines the reception of his work by
critics. Susan Rather, Smithsonian Fellow, explores the archaic and
classical Greek sources which formed the basis of his early work between
1910-1930 and analyzes East Indian influences in Manship's work.
Gurdon L. Tarbox, Jr., and Robin R. Salmon, Brookgreen Gardens,
include a historical account of garden sculpture and discuss Manship's
works at Brookgreen and the artist's role in garden sculpture. Dr. William
M. Stott, The University of Texas, Austin, explores Manship's
contributions and assesses the changing socio-political, economic and
cultural milieus which contributed to his decline, or perceived decline,

among tastemakers and critics of American art. John Manship, in his essay of biographical recollections, gives an intimate and revealing view of his father, and the times in which they lived.

While not all-inclusive, the exhibition and catalogue are retrospective in the sense that they look back over his work and career, both in a linear and thematic way. Where possible drawings and sculptural sketches are placed in proximity and compared to the final works.

By working in the classical mode, Manship has eluded currents of fashion, and his work remains solidly anchored in time.

Gloria Kittleson
Curator of Collections

7. Isidore Konti (1862-1938)
Dancing Figure, 1910
bronze
11¾ high
Collection Montclair Art Museum,
Montclair, New Jersey
Gift of Edward Dufner, 1937

Following his study with Charles Grafly in 1907-1908 at the Pennsylvania Academy of Fine Arts, Paul Manship served as an assistant to Konti from 1908-1909. Under Konti's tutelage, Manship became more like a son than an assistant to the sculptor.* It was Konti who persuaded Manship to enter the competition for the American Academy in Rome. Manship's relief sculpture, *Rest After Toil,* took first place. (Interestingly enough, Konti had won a similar prize for two years of study in Rome during his own student days in Vienna.) The two men shared a love of classical sculpture and remained close friends until Konti's death in 1938.

In the early 1890s, Konti had served as assistant to Karl Bitter, also Viennese born. Bitter's admiration for Greek classical art was absorbed by Konti and, indirectly, may have influenced Manship's interest in the subject. Bitter's archaic Greek style may be seen in his carved relief pediments at the Wisconsin State Capitol, completed in 1908-1910.

Classical influences are evident in *Dancing Figure,* a prime example of Konti's decorative, idealized style. A small, dainty female figure is balanced on her right foot, her left leg crossed to the front with foot raised, as for a dance step. Swirling draperies form a backdrop for the figure, and her right hand holds a fold of cloth to her breast, while her left hand partially controls the drapery folds. Her head is bent slightly backward and to the right side. The work is decorative and appears to be a study for a garden or fountain figure, for which Konti had received many commissions throughout his successful career, as did Manship.

*The Hudson River Museum, *The Sculpture of Isadore Konti 1862-1938* (Yonkers, N.Y.: The Hudson River Museum, 1975), 5, unpaginated introduction.
J.F.H.
G.K.

Solon H. Borglum (1868-1922)
8. *Evening*, 1905
bronze
22 x 24 x 8½
Courtesy Solon Borglum Sculpture Project

Fig. 2
Pulling, c. 1906
(lost work)

It was as a student of Solon Borglum, the great animal sculptor, that Manship learned the grasp of anatomy. Borglum was avid about his students understanding the basic structure underlying forms, and in 1920 opened a school where these principles were part of the curriculum, and also wrote a book on the subject entitled *Sound Constructions* (published posthumously in 1923).

Famous for his equestrian statuary, Borglum was working on two such monuments when Manship was his assistant; one of these was the *Rough Rider* Bucky O'Neill monument. Manship studied with Borglum from spring 1905 to October 1907.* These years were significant as Manship was learning anatomy through the dissection of horses and dogs under Borglum's guidance, on their visits to the vets and the morgue.

In *Evening*, Borglum captures the mood and feeling of the rugged American West. He had studied in Paris briefly at the Académie Julian, and the French called him the "poet of the Western Prairie," but Borglum remained truly American, never adopting the Beaux-Arts style.

Similar to *Evening* is a work by Manship, *End of Day*, 1909, with its rough surfaces, which shows the influence

of Borglum in subject, compositional format and surface treatment. Manship also completed a plaster study *Pulling* (Fig. 2) 1906, known only through photographs, of a group of horses pulling a sand scoop. This work was a great satisfaction to both Manship and Borglum,

and showed Manship's understanding of the lessons Borglum was imparting to him.
*A Mervyn Davies, *Solon H. Borglum "A Man Who Stands Alone"* (Chester, Conn., Pequot Press, 1974), 140.
G.K.

The Stature of Paul Manship

9. *Lyric Muse*, 1912
bronze, marble base
13⅞ x 10¼ x 7
66.14.02
Murtha 19

In classical Greek mythology, the nine
goddesses who inspired creativity in
literature, art and sciences were called the
Muses. Two of the Muses historically are
termed "lyric." Euterpe has been
designated the Muse of lyric poetry and
music, her attribute being the flute. Erato
has been called the Muse of both lyric and
love poetry, as well as mime, her attribute
being the lyre.* Since Manship's *Lyric Muse*
holds a lyre, she probably represents Erato.
The muse has almond-shaped eyes, and her
hair falls over her shoulders in evenly
arranged strands of stylized curls, held in
place by a fillet wound around her head.
Manship adapted these stylizations of eyes
and hair from female figures in archaic
Greek and Etruscan art. In 1916, Manship
illustrated the figure of *Lyric Muse* again on
the observe of the *Saint Paul Art Institute
Medal* (66.14.233).
*James Hall, *A History of Ideas and Images
in Italian Art* (New York, Harper & Row,
1983), 60.
L.A.K.
S.L.

Paul Manship's formal competence, even his genuine virtuosity appear
unnoticeable against the titanic contemporary development of Cubism —
the greatest deflection in the course of Western sculpture's evolution since
the Renaissance. This least predictable and subsequently most fecund
achievement of modern sculpture was Picasso's triumph, for, if Braque was
Picasso's equal as a painter, Picasso's sculptural experiments were unrivaled
in any medium by a modern artist — except perhaps by his own dexterity
as a printmaker. Relative to the gigantic accomplishments of European
modernism and later, in America, by the Abstract Expressionists, the
chronicle of this century might well disregard Manship. Rightfully, his
work could be relegated to the ranks of first-rate artisans, were it not for
the art historical importance of the synthesis that Manship forged — a
legitimate response to the conditions that propelled modernism itself —
and the technical fluency of his treatment. Yet, even that assessment
proves partial, lacking an account of the most meaningful contribution of
his art — formal originality almost without equal.

Among the international formalists that included Ernst Barlach,
Wilhelm Lehmbruck, and Carl Milles, Paul Howard Manship was an
equal. From 1939 until 1942, Manship was President of the National
Sculpture Society, and from 1948 to 1954 he was President of the
National Academy of Arts and Letters.¹ Nevertheless, in the post-war era
Manship's conservatism and apparent affiliation with Art Deco — an
artistic vocabulary he helped create but whose decorative program he never
endorsed — caused his immense reputation to totter and his once
unparalleled personal influence to evaporate. To succeeding generations of
sculptors he was a ghostly figure, whose representative work, if consulted
at all, consisted of certain prominent monuments whose scale of
opportunity was envied by the young but whose style was abhorrent to
them. Over the course of Manship's career his work became grander, but
no more abstract. Indeed, for him, *abstraction* was not an alluring country
to venture into; abstraction was not the telos of modern art. Absent from
his work is any notion of grand artistic progress beyond the individual
attainment of dexterity. Indeed, among Manship and his most successful
contemporaries the critical difference lay in just that absence of an
overview of his art within the context of art history. A student of

sculpture, Manship's self-education in the humanities predisposed him to uncertainty about his intellectual credentials and, while he worked assiduously to tutor himself — learning French and Italian as well as the intricacies of mythology, upon which he founded his imagery — the sense that great artists display, of naturally *possessing* history as their rightful inheritance was never his.[2] His Midwestern heritage of blunt forthrightness, and his own sense of place in the modern world rendered Manship a transitional figure, upon whose heritage none could ever rightly build. His sculpture seems tangential to the course of art history, an original comment on the formal possibilities of the figure with no intrinsic agenda that invited others to assume his style or to advance it beyond what he had done.

When Manship died in January 1966 at the age of eighty-one he had witnessed a revolution in abstract sculpture that he reviled and against which he had unsuccessfuly fought. To post-war artists Manship seemed an uncomfortably looming figure who, although a giant in his own time, could easily be side-stepped or preferably ignored rather than reconciled with the development of modern sculpture; indeed, this proved to be the sadly accurate consensus among artists whose personal art histories — by which they navigated toward their own goals — less and less frequently featured Manship.

For fully a generation, the public recalled Manship's work as, at best, a mere footnote or a lovely impressive curiosity. In recent years a reconsideration of Art Deco has revived his reputation — which should never have suffered demotion. His centenary now affords the moment for a celebration of his work.

In the period between the wars Manship epitomized the best features of American conservativism, or academic sculpture, which he had helped to reform and invigorate. Without his knowing it, and before the term was coined, Manship participated in the formation of our era's most popular and long-lived style of art and decoration, Art Deco.[3] It is impossible to discuss his career without referring to some aspect of this style — regardless of what name or by which features one addresses it. So widespread is its occurrence, so frequent its revival in different guises, and so beloved is it by public and designers alike that, much as we name

10. *Detail from Stained Glass Window, Poitiers,* 1922
pencil on paper
14¹⁄₁₆ x 9 ¹¹⁄₁₆ (sheet)
1966.47.214
National Museum of American Art,
Smithsonian Institution
Gift of the Estate of Paul Manship

In 1922, Manship traveled in France with his friend and colleague, Barry Faulkner. On 7 September, he was in Poitiers, a city in west central France. This drawing is a study from a stained glass window of a medieval cathedral.

This study depicts an enthroned figure. Manship has clearly captured the feeling of restless, up-and-down movement in Romanesque gestures. The two-dimensional, linear composition of the figure is also enlivened by a similar sense of movement.

In this drawing Manship appears to have been concentrating primarily on the problems involved in portraying a three-dimensional seated figure within the restrictive confines of a two-dimensional space. He had already designed human figures in limestone for the rectangular niches of the Pierpont Morgan Memorial in 1920 (Fig. 3); in 1934, he would confront similar spatial problems when designing the bear and deer groups for the bronze grillwork arches of the Paul J. Rainey Memorial Gateway (Fig. 11).

Manship seems to have been intrigued by the manner in which the stained glass artists of medieval France fitted portions of the figure into the small, irregularly-shaped window sections reserved for them.
L.A.K.
S.L.

different archaeological strata by their prevalent styles as their artifacts re-emerge into the light, our century will probably be remembered by this period style. Art Deco reconciled art and industry; it incorporated modernist-inspired form, academic formalisms and literary references, citations from antiquity, and a rakish love of speed that typified the modern era and recalled the energetic expressions of Futurism — itself the spawn of Cubism. These sources merged into a consistent fashion with the potential for universal application in textiles, buildings, graphic design, household utensils and garments. A type of modern art indigenous to this era, Art Deco — which expressed admiration for streamlined machine shapes — might have grown up independent of other forms of modernism; evolutionary in its accounting of the whole built environment, Art Deco

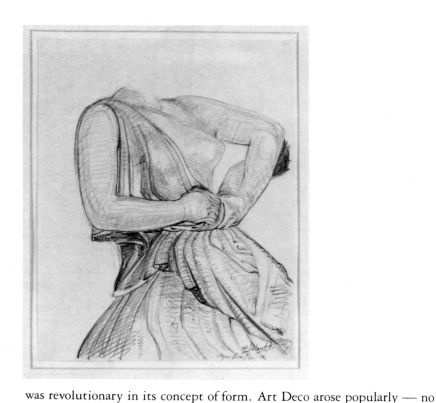

11. *Detail of Figure from Olympia,* 1924
pencil on paper
12¾ x 10
Collection Michael Birdsall and
Roger Haase

This drawing of Olympia may have been
made from a reconstruction of the west
pediment of the Temple of Zeus at
Olympia (470-450 B.C.), which Manship
could have seen in the Museum at
Olympia. The theme of the west pediment
is the wedding feast of Peirithoös where
centaurs are celebrating wildly and, in this
case, a centaur, Euarytion, whom we don't
see, is attempting to seize the bride,
Deidameia. Manship has captured the
momentary effect of the young maiden
being pulled away by the centaur, and her
resistance to him with the opposing
movement and tortion of her body. The
archaic accordion-like folds of the drapery
contrast with the young and tender body,
combining to make a graceful turning
form.
G.K.

was revolutionary in its concept of form. Art Deco arose popularly — no
manifesto, program or declaration issued from a coterie to mark its
beginnings. It succeeded where the eminent Bauhaus theoreticians failed;
it created a style appropriate to every type of human dwelling or dress.
Manship never advocated this style; the formulation of his artistic goals
and style predated both his tremendous artistic stature and any stylistic
association with Art Deco. Nevertheless, he advocated the creation of a
new sculpture that would harmonize with the flow of the modern world as
a fitting component of the new architecture, its buildings, parks, plazas
and rising cityscapes.

Planning on such a scale required access to centers of power and the
pivotal personalities of the age. Manship's workmanlike personality
predisposed him to mingle with tycoons; his business sense endeared him
to architects; his unchallenging, politically neutral imagery recommended
itself to municipal planners.

Manship's earliest works faintly indicate those tendencies that later
developed into the major traits of his sculpture. A *Self-Portrait* (1) 1906-
1907, in warm-toned monochrome washes suggests the youth's color-
blindness which led him to choose sculpture as his medium. For most of
his subsequent career polychromy was not a component of Manship's art,
and when it appeared, it featured only incidentally as minor passages
within major works, or in the choice of some rare and beautiful material
whose unaltered substance contrasted with bronze. In heroically scaled

12. *Lion of St. Marc, Moissac*, 1922
pencil on paper
14 x 9⅜
66.14.136

Manship visited the south of France in 1922 and sketched Romanesque sculpture from the south portal of the Cathedral of St. Pierre at Moissac. On 18 September he sketched the lion representing Saint Mark.

In medieval art, the evangelists were conventionally symbolized by beasts from the Apocalypse. The winged lion symbolizes Saint Mark and is often seen flanking the figures of Christ in the company of the other Evangelists.

Manship may have been intrigued by the resemblance of the winged lion of Saint Mark to his own sculpted griffins, creatures which are part lion and part bird. Before visiting Moissac, Manship sculpted two griffins for Charles Schwab's garden in Pennsylvania; he also included two griffins on his *Cycle of Life-Armillary Sphere* (89).

The position of the lion's head, turned unnaturally toward his back, and the mane of the animal were stylistic observations Manship would use in his later works, e.g. the animals in *Diana* (45) and *Actaeon* (46). S.L.

versions of some of his most successful works Manship added touches of polychromy, almost always to the detriment of the work's clarity. His predeliction for monochromatic conception of form would stand him in good stead among the practitioners of Art Deco, in which surface pattern triumphed over ornamentation based on changes in hue. Although this general taste grew from wide-scale preference for a machine-age aesthetic, Manship's needs and that of the general taste converged. The artist was in an *avant-garde* of popular sensibility; he saw art performing a social and humanizing function. Later in his career his commissions satisfied a clientele whose expectations were based upon his own earlier works — a situation that stymied the maturation of a late, masterful, style.

Manship never knowingly served any master but his own sense of a workmanlike job, and his reputation, which was built upon his artisanship; his attention to craftsmanship predominated throughout his life. Precisely this distinction between the artisan and the modernist/experimenter separated Manship from the most advanced thinking of his age. That on numerous occasions he surpassed his own standards and achieved real formal innovation and virtuosity only confused the matter. If he succeeded within the restrictive terms he had set, others also could, and he held young artists accountable; yet, his program had arisen in response to a specific artistic situation that no longer prevailed after the earliest days of his career, and certainly after World War II the situation had changed. Manship felt that his product would not challenge the

13. *Playfulness*, 1912
bronze, marble base
13⅛ x 12⅝ x 7
National Museum of American Art,
Smithsonian Institution
Gift of Paul Manship
1965.16.12
Murtha 21

Playfulness depicts a young woman playing
with a baby. She leans backward on the
stool, rocking the child on her knee, while
holding its small arms securely in both
hands. A similar sculpture, *Little Brother*
(Murtha 18), shows the same model
holding the child upright, positioned near
her right shoulder. Unlike *Little Brother*, in
which both figures are momentarily still,
Playfulness is full of movement. Both works
were completed in Rome at the same time
as *Lyric Muse* (9) 1912. All three sculptures
exhibit similar archaic stylizations. Eyes
are almond-shaped, hair tightly arranged
and bodies are smooth-surfaced. The
woman's sharply-pleated garment, which
spills over the stool, suggests drapery
conventions employed by archaic Greek,
Etruscan and Indian artists. Unlike *Lyric
Muse*, however, *Playfulness* and *Little Brother*
are purely domestic in theme, and display
engaging touches of naturalism. For
example, in *Playfulness*, the folds in the
woman's abdomen and her wiggling toes
are realistically portrayed. The child's
chubby, wildly kicking legs and soft,
protruding stomach are also charming,
true-to-life details.
L.A.K.
S.L.

assumptions by which society was ordered, and would enhance the
humanist tradition at its core. Naturally, such a position was easily
misunderstood and at times willfully misconstrued when his work fell out
of fashion. Manship retaliated with anger against the newer generation of
artists who inclined toward abstraction, and a natural chain of artistic
pedigree was thus sundered. It was maintained only by Lachaise and
Nakian — particularly by the former whose work shows a strong
structural debt to Manship's way of massing figures.

Evidence of Manship's willfully unbending integrity appears in his
earliest works. In the early *Self-Portrait* his serious, but unsolemn gaze
testifies to the earnest pursuit of art, career and reputation that was typical
of him throughout his life. Sureness of form, characteristic of the sculptor's
best drawings is amply apparent in this straightforward and solid
rendition. Perhaps even at this date Manship was aware of how form is
draped over an armature, a preference that attracted him to cast in bronze,
which begins as a sheath above underlying support.

During Manship's three-year scholarship at the American Academy in
Rome he fell under the direct spell of a classicism that invigorated his
work thereafter. The allure of the antique appealed both to Manship's
discomfort with modernism's severity and Expressionism's arbitrary
distortions. Neither cerebral purity — an approach that elevated
conception above perception, thought above beauty — nor the excesses of
unpredictable invention suited him. During the first decade of this
century Manship struggled with the same range of artistic problems that
engrossed his contemporaries. His solution to a personal artistic dilemma
predated what others later chose but, subsequently, many artists selected
the course he charted between what seemed two equally unappealing
extremes. By 1911 he had mastered a vivacious revival style of Roman
bronze-work. His attraction to the past evidenced reaction, although he
never exactly copied antiquity. This immensely talented young man's
reinterpretation of inherited values resulted in a sculpture that combined
the ductile quality of molten metal, with its liquid gestural potential, its
opportunity for detail expressed as ornament and its surface treatment of
chased metal surfaces as a sensuous component independent of subject
matter.

14. *Europa and the Bull*, 1924-1935
bronze
24 x 39 x 15
66.14.42
Murtha 354

According to myth, Zeus fell in love with Europa, the beautiful daughter of Agenor, King of Phoenicia, and devised a plan to possess her. He sent Hermes to drive Agenor's cattle to the seashore where Europa and her companions were playing. Zeus then changed himself into a magnificent white bull and mingled among the cattle grazing near Europa. At

In 1912 Manship produced *Lyric Muse* (9), a sculpture that heralds his dawning artistic independence — and admittedly represents an odd sort of autonomy when compared with contemporary developments, like nascent Cubism. Each element in this work subtly cites some past artistic tradition. Modeled completely in the round, the figure is highlighted by areas of archaistic surface pattern limited to hair and drapery. These passages graphically balance the accents of geometric ornament and smooth surfaces. Despite temptations to treat forms as a carefully balanced design originating in linear plan, Manship always conceived his works sculpturally. The spiral body of the *Lyric Muse* is a fully spatial concept that does not rely upon or resolve into a pattern projected upon a flat plane. In a traditional sense the work is conceived as a response to the demands of anatomical truth, a clear statement of formal postulates, and first she was frightened of the bull but gradually lost her fear, played about him and even put garlands of flowers on his horns. Finally Europa got on the back of the animal. Slowly, with Europa still on his back, the bull made his way to the shore, plunged into the sea and swam off. Arriving in Crete, Zeus shed his disguise and revealed his divine identity to Europa. She eventually bore him three sons: Minos, Rhadamanthys and Sarpedon.

In the larger version of *Europa and the Bull* (14) Manship depicts Europa seated on the ground in front of the reclining bull, obviously enchanted with the animal. Her arms reach up and back to embrace the bull's head, and her forehead and back rest gently against his massive body. The bull's mouth is slightly open, and his tongue lightly touches Europa's inner arm, just above the elbow. An aura of sensuality emanates from the fully-contoured bodies of the animal and the maiden. The feeling is further intensified by the sculptor's resolution of their formal interrelationships. Compositionally, the grouping is based on a series of closely interlocking triangles, which lends stability and a sense of three-dimensional monumentality to the work.

MMA owns a small maquette of *Europa and the Bull*, 1922 (66.14.79), a study for the larger work. (A mid-size group of *Europa and the Bull* is owned by Walker Art Center).

L.A.K.
S.L.

an exercise in bronze's textural mimicry of smooth skin. Gesturally, the singer's open mouth seems an amplification of the slightly parted lips of antique sculpture, and the open mouths of Baroque sculpture — perhaps itself an excessive exploitation of antiquity. Manship, the autodidact, hoped his spectators appreciated the classical references in his work, and, however esoteric, his subjects never described novel combinations but rather represented certifiable, if obscure, passages of classical literature — a crucial distinction, as he wished not to be thought ignorant on these points. In this manner he established what no diplomas or certification could bestow — his legitimate access to what archaeology had unearthed and scholarship reconstructed. He exploited the past, mining antiquity's treasures of its formal possibilities. He successfully adapted classical and oriental antiquity, the passport of his knowledge always visible, displayed to gain his spectator's confidence.

The *Lyric Muse* recalls a long lineage of "Erato" statues — the Muse of hymns or lyric poetry. In an unbroken stream reaching back into antiquity this figure appeared in similar — if less sculpturally sophisticated — poses, inspiring bards and poets who celebrated the Muses as among the most benign and lovely creations of myth. The Muses inculcated wisdom, brought purifying music, inspired poetry and personified the highest intellectual achievement. Hesiod was responsible for naming the Muses and fixing their canonical number at nine; later, the Romans distinguished their individual functions, and Horace penned lines to which Manship's figure might have been responding as she rises, having just plucked her lyre:

> But if you give me a place among the bards of the lyre,
> I shall lift up my head till it strikes the stars. [1]

Once having mastered this spiral form Manship frequently employed it with success. It appears within the compactly massed *Europa and the Bull* (14) 1924-35, a work that seems in dialogue with two of Lachaise's sculptures: *Woman in Chair (With Right Arm Raised)*, 1924, [Hirshhorn Museum] and the denser *The Mountain*, (executed in versions from c. 1913-1934). Unusual for its spatial opacity, such an interpretation of the helix shows how innately Manship understood the potential of the form. Throughout his career Manship used a cylindrical curve, as, in the open and airy *Icarus Falling* (24) 1965, a later work that swirls and tumbles like a falling leaf. He learned control of the closed columnar form, which he used to marvelous advantage depicting that moment when, alighting from the surf and washing the ocean from her hair, *Venus Anadyomene* (62) 1924, first steps on land.

Not all of Manship's ambitions relied on classical or biblical formulations; his work of 1926, *Indian Hunter and His Dog* (95), in which he availed himself of new world subject matter, may depend on the precedent of John Quincy Adams Ward's *Indian Hunter,* 1864, [New York Historical Society, New York.] Likewise, he was a master of animal sculpture, the nude male figure, children, and the openwork of screens or armillary spheres and sundials. The wonderful composition of the *Time and the Fates Sundial* (80) for the 1939 New York World's Fair effortlessly combines the most esoteric citations into a functional object. As executed the figures were heroically scaled. His strongest works — those small pieces modeled in clay that could be held in the hand, and which displayed the sculptor's feel for his materials — were never successfully enlarged. The level of detail is satisfactory, indeed entrancing, in the miniatures; in the large works, by comparison, it becomes vacant, pychologically blank. The monumental pieces appear somewhat bloated, and Manship never reconciled absolute size with monumental conception. Yet, for pure formal invention he had few genuine rivals, so long as he worked for himself. For example, *Baboon* (56) 1932, a sketchy, unsurpassable drawing, is breathtaking in its concision, accuracy and elegance. It reminds us of the best sort of drawings done by sculptors, those works in which volume assumes an easy familiarity. Yet, for all his mastery of the technical and formal qualities of sculpture, his work — an art of precise outlines, clarity and balance — seemed strangely aloof from the world that moved around him.

There is no evidence in Manship's art that Freud ever lived. His female figures pose with the healthy titillating innocence of nudist camp devotees (the same sort of gratuitous eroticism that *Playboy* centerfolds epitomized for so long); they lack that mystery of archaic Mediterranean sculpture which so hauntingly evokes the primordial discovery of gender. His well-muscled males possess none of the quivering tautness of antique sculpture.

15. *Flight of Europa*, 1925
gilded bronze, marble base
22⅛ x 31 x 7¾
National Museum of American Art,
Smithsonian Institution
Gift of Paul Manship
1965.16.26
Murtha 177

The bull in this grouping resembles the
Minoan bull frescoes from the Palace of
Minos at Knossos; Manship toured the
island of Crete in the early 1920s. The
large heavily-muscled animal rushes
forward through the waves, escorted by
four dolphins. Europa sits primly upon his

back, her head facing backwards. Her legs
are casually crossed, and she seems totally
unconcerned about her kidnapping. Eros,
the Greek god of love, balanced on tiptoe
on the bull's arched neck, whispers
encouragement in her ear.

Despite the presence of Eros, the
sensual warmth that humanizes Manship's
1924-1935 version of Europa's abduction
(14), is absent here. A sense of playfulness
animates these lively silhouettes; the
humor in the situation is further enhanced
by the antics of the sporty dolphin convoy.
L.A.K.
J.F.H.

The figures of *Diana* (45) 1921, and *Actaeon* (46) 1923, hardly note the fundamental isometry of male and female as mythological avatars; the resulting sculptural solution is more eloquent in pure form, and in period style than in human terms. Indeed, compared with what most "modern" sculptors were then doing, the purely sculptural quality of Manship's conception of *Diana* is staggering for its total command of spatial organization. What his interpretation of this theme lacks is any indication of the urges underlying the myth. Manship's clientele discouraged public salutes to overt sex, and should any such display have tinged his art, the intrusion would almost certainly have hurt his trade in monumental commissions. Likewise, *Atalanta* (67) 1921, acquits herself unselfconsciously, not as a nearly naked lady but as perhaps the most daring open circular composition until David Smith's *Circle* sculptures forty years later. Manship himself lived normally and healthily amid wife and children. His family appears intermittently in works that seem strictly personal and occasional. (These pieces of purely factual reportage, are, frankly among the least successful of his long career.) Yet, in direct competition with his genuinely academic contemporaries, even Manship's limited depth of intuitive human understanding stands clear. His gilded 1926 version of the *Flight of Europa* (15), National Museum of American Art, levitates the solid mass of the bull (Zeus) carrying the Phoenician princess; charging westward, accompanied by leaping dolphins, a cherub whispers to Europa who, intoxicated by the situation, sits, gazing toward the distant horizon of the ocean. Simultaneously, Carl Milles, who had worked in Rodin's studio, executed the same theme, with very different results [bronze model, 31½", Cranbrook Academy of Art Museum]. For Milles, the animal, with legs folded beneath it — a static mass directly supported by the ground — arches backward in a single animating gesture toward the outstretched figure of Europa (a Hellenistic conflation) and licks her hand. Compared to this blunt attempt at eroticism, Manship's adult sensuality swells the revelation of female triumph. That Manship's human insights are not his greatest strength does not sufficiently distinguish him from contemporary academics whose own work in comparison appears almost irredeemably dull.

Manship's imagination never strayed into a fantasy world such as the idiosyncratic realm discovered in the wake of psychoanalysis; his images do not issue either from his autobiography (in any obvious way) nor from the "unconscious." Significantly, Manship's subjects are conventional, all have names that can be found in books, usually those on classical mythology, and for him these primordial mythological treatments sufficed as occasions to expound on human relationships. Perhaps early success inured him against soul-searching, or his workmanlike approach precluded the "frivolity" of the more extreme forms of self-expression. In his art we find nothing confessional. Although staunchly figurative, and something of a Romantic by modern standards, Manship did not indulge in phantasmagoria, although he maintained a Parisian studio while the Surrealists founded their movement.

There, inevitably, Manship came under Rodin's forceful presence, against whose influence he struggled early and successfully. Rodin's expressive, unsystematic sculpture could be neither delegated to, nor inherited by a succeeding generation; it represented the gigantic outpouring of an enormous personality. Rodin's unpredictable sculpture offered heroic possibilities, but also held the liability of a bathetic chasm which is evident in the master's less successful moments.

Manship helped produce another alternative, remote from Rodin's instruction, and sprung from a different stream of speculation. An heir to ninteenth century Romantic exoticism Manship rallied diverse sources from antiquity and the Orient, convening their most elegant formal achievements in a meeting of styles that never debased itself into a medley. Instead, he achieved a careful new amalgam without adulturine citation. Regardless of how his audience received his work, Manship treated his influences with respect, not as exotic curios from a mystical and misunderstood past. He shared something of early modernism's eclecticism for pre-classical cultures. But Manship eschewed primitivism, both for its symbolic incoherence and for its formal disintegration. These very traits appealed to the inquisitive modernists and beckoned to the youthful Picasso and Matisse from the Trocadèro — eventually the *avant-garde*'s inoculation of primitivism toppled the edifice of traditional Western art. For Manship, the recapitulation, yet again, but with a novel vigor and authentic modernity, of the classical world held out rich promises too

16. *Europa,* 1928
porcelain
16 x 19 x 10
Collection Cowan Pottery Museum
Rocky River, Ohio
cf. Murtha 190

This is the only known Manship porcelain
work on this subject. Although little is
known about Manship's involvement with
the Cowan Pottery Company, he did work
for the company and produced some
designs for ceramics in the late 1920s.

Murtha indicates that Manship
produced glazed terra cotta Europas in
various colors; these also may have been
completed at the Cowan pottery Museum.

The complete figure of *Europa* is
transferred almost without change from
the bronze sculpture of 1924 to the
porcelain piece of 1928.
J.F.H.

great to reject summarily.

The rigorous, hermetic and rationally formal realm of Cubism (even its humor concerns reflexive jokes about art), produced a serenity akin to, but different from, that toward which Manship strove. He viewed himself as a legitimate heir to the legacy of all of Western art. So ordained, Manship produced a synthesis that concluded the history of pre-modern art, even while offering an alternative. His was a sculpture about sculpture's history, as much as Cubism produced a sculpture about sculpture. Manship's art represented the memory of sculpture rather than a rediscovery.

His was a meta-sculpture, peculiarly suited to, and a victim of, that moment when sophistication first became universally available. Manship's work might have summarized the character and development of art from the eighteenth century to his own day, except for his conspicuous exclusion of the major contemporary intellectual and artistic developments. So much of modern art — generated by the Cubists, Surrealists, modern formalists, Dada theoreticians, psychoanalytic investigators — found no welcome in his sculpture, and, cut off from so many fresh streams of inquiry, he found it difficult to keep his art vital. Manship worked from an essentially fixed agenda that altered little during his long career. His sculpture, which fully addressed the great questions of the new century, paralleled the other characteristic expressions of our time as a response to the art of the nineteenth century. His art thus represents an alternative channel, if a limited one, to the other great artistic explorations of our age. But within these self-imposed limits he succeeded to the fullest possible extent. Surpassing the academic norms, Manship was no atavism, but a legitimate, if unexpected, personality in the stream of twentieth century art. As such he is entitled to unprejudiced evaluation, a judgment that must result in admiration and an appreciation of his often breathtaking accomplishments.

Harry Rand
Curator, Painting and Sculpture
National Museum of American Art,
Smithsonian Institution

17. *Nude Female with Putto and*
Dolphins, n.d.
pencil on board
15⅝ x 9¼
Collection Mr. and Mrs.
Thomond R. O'Brien

The Birth of Aphrodite, the Greek
goddess of love and beauty, from the foam
of the sea may be the subject of this pencil
drawing. The nude young woman, her
body arching gracefully like the slow curl
of a wave, appears to be emerging from the
water, which is symbolically represented
by the leaping dolphins at her feet. The
putto is possibly Aphrodite's son, Eros.

   The position of the woman's arms,
extended languorously above her head,
slightly bent at the wrists and elbows, is
similar to Manship's depiction of Europa
in *Europa and the Bull* (14), and to a small
study of *Europa and the Bull* in MMA's
collection (66.14.79), which shows the
Phoenician princess embracing the bull's
head in this manner. Dolphins and a putto
also accompany her in *Flight of Europa*
(15). The fact that the woman is totally
nude also suggests that she may represent
Aphrodite.
L.A.K.
S.L.

Notes

1

Recognition came early to Manship. After his Roman sojourn (1909-1912) he was elected to the National Academy of Design in 1916; soon thereafter he was elected to the National Sculpture Society and the Architectural League of New York. He was elected to the National Institute of Arts and Letters in 1920, in 1931 to the American Academy of Arts and Sciences, and in 1932 to the American Academy of Arts and Letters; in that same year he became a member of the Smithsonian Institution's Art Commission and served on that body for forty-three years, for twenty as its chairman.

2

After a short career as a designer in Saint Paul, Manship left high school rather than be ejected for failing grades. In early 1905 he entered the Art Students League and then served as an assistant to Solon Borglum from 1905-1907, followed by study with Charles Grafly at the Pennsylvania Academy of Fine Arts in Philadelphia. He assisted Isidore Konti in 1908-1909 and was a pupil of Jo Davidson. Manship and Hunt Diedrich visited Spain in 1907.

3

The style, while generally recognizable after the briefest familiarity, has gone by many titles; one source, summarizing the situation, lists twenty-six different names (Bevis Hillier, *Art Deco of the 20s and 30s,* Dutton, 1968).

4

Horace, *Odes,* bk. 1, see 1, 35.

5

The theme enjoyed a momentary flash of attention among traditional sculptors; Waylande Gregory essayed the possibilities of *Europa and the Bull* between 1937-1938 in a large stoneware sculpture [Everson Museum of Art]. Between 1938-1942 Reuben Nakian modelled a version of the subject as well. And David Smith, conjectured on the results of this amorous elopement in *Europa and Calf* [National Museum of American Art] which foreshadows the planar arrangement of a work named for his daughter, *Becca.* [Metropolitan Museum].

Fig. 3
John Pierpont Morgan Memorial Tablet, 1920
limestone (Champville)
11'2" x 5'4"
Designed by Paul Manship, and executed
by Gaston Lachaise and Paul Manship,
Collection The Metropolitan Museum of
Art, New York
Murtha 122

The *John Pierpont Morgan Memorial* was one
of Manship's first important commissions.
In 1914, the artist was chosen by the
trustees of The Metropolitan Museum of
Art to execute a memorial honoring the
late President of the museum. The
monument is in the form of a stone tablet.
Its present location is on the southeast wall
of the vestibule of the main Fifth Avenue
entrance.

The memorial consists of a large central
inscription panel flanked by three vertical
niches on each side and by horizontal
niches above and below. The six vertical
allegorical niche figures represent the
interests of J. P. Morgan: commerce,
finance, science, art, literature and
archaeology. In the upper horizontal niche,
there are two winged putti with trumpets,
flanked by griffins. Manship described the
male and female figures playing lyres in
the lower horizontal niche "in attitudes of
extolling and lamenting."* On the sides of
the monument, not visible in the
photograph, are signs of the zodiac in low
relief symbolizing, according to Manship,
the "Cycle of the Year or the Compass of
Life."
*Bulletin of The Metropolitan Museum of
Art, 15 (1920), 267.
S.L.

36

18. *Science*, 1913
pencil on paper
8⅝ x 4
66.14.137f

19. *Literature*, 1913
pencil on paper
8½ x 3¼
66.14.137c

20. *Archaeology*, 1913
pencil on paper
7¾ x 3⅛
66.14.137h

21. *Finance*, 1913
pencil on paper
8 x 3½
66.14.137b

Although Manship was not commissioned
to execute the John Pierpont Memorial
until 1914, he started making studies for
the work in 1913. These four drawings are
studies for four of the six vertical niche
figures: *Finance* and *Science* are on the left
side of the tablet, and *Literature* and
Archaeology are on the right side. *Finance* is
symbolized by a crowned woman holding a
cornucopia, symbolic of abundance, in her
left hand and a staff in her right hand.
Science is depicted as a man holding a globe
and a flask, symbolizing astronomy and
chemistry. The figure of *Literature* appears
as a classical philosopher with a laurel
wreath on his head holding an open book.
Archaeology is represented as a classically-
draped female figure holding a column and
an antique vase. In the memorial
tablet, male and female figures alternate,
balancing the composition.
S.L.

38

Paul Manship: Artist, Time and Place

22. *Adam*, 1925
gilded bronze, marble base
18⅞ x 5⅝ x 5⅝
66.14.66a
Murtha 184

In *Adam* and *Eve,* we see Manship's tendency in the 1920s to represent the figure in more fulsome, powerful volumes, a marked change from the delicate archaic figures of the teens. The biblical themes may possibly be combined here: *Adam* depicts the Temptation, as he contemplates the apple, not yet having eaten of the fruit, and is flanked by a dog with its connotation of fidelity; *Eve* (23) is portrayed later in the Expulsion from the Garden scene, with her head buried in her arm as she turns to the side and looks down at the serpent with the face of a woman, entwined around her foot, symbolizing deceit.

These salon figures provided Manship an opportunity to present the theme with realism combined with a sense of classical proportion. An earlier pair of *Adam* and *Eve,* 1922, is in MMA's collection (66.14.29a and b; Murtha 151 and 152). Manship also completed candlesticks with this motif (Murtha 78).
G.K.

The life and art of Paul H. Manship (1885-1966) clearly reflect the dominant values of the United States in the period between the two great wars; the fact that culture, position and wealth were all but synonymous helped but did not determine his astonishingly successful career. At its beginning in 1916, it was said: " 'The cultured people of this generation almost instantly recognized Manship to be *their* sculptor. They get from him what they would get in surgery from the best surgeon of the day and in engineering from the best engineer, and so on.' "[1] Manship seems to have been aware of this: "I was the right man at the right time."[2] Indeed, he was even more perceptive than that: he specified the time, between 1915 and 1940: "That was a good period, that twenty-five years. I sold many, many small bronzes — pieces I made for my own pleasure and not for commissions."[3] The enormity of his sales, whether of commissioned works or not, corroborates the concordance of artist and patrons, and of the values they shared.

Manship's friend and art critic for the *New York Herald-Tribune,* Royal Cortissoz, touched upon this unanimity of artist and patron in 1933 in an hitherto unremarked and telling estimate of the sculptor's work which was "...so exactly fitted to the requirements of the nation which produced it."[4] A quick reading of this sentence allows it as simple praise; however, a second reading makes the antecedent of the pronoun quite unclear, ambivalent at best. Was the sculpture produced by Manship, or by the nation? Was this sentence a slip of the pen or a precise detailing of the relationship existing between the artist and the nation, his public? Did the critic intend to represent the sculptor as an agent, so to speak, of the nation, or at least of those leaders who embodied the values of the nation? It is quite possible the latter was the case. Leon Trotsky (1877-1940), paradoxically a more conservative critic than Royal Cortissoz, speaks of the artist-patron relationship and makes Cortissoz' implication explicit:

The truth is that even if individuality is unique, it does not mean that it cannot be analysed. Individuality is a welding together of tribal, national, class, temporary, and institutional elements, and, in fact it is the uniqueness of this welding together, in the proportions of this psychochemical mixture, that individuality is expressed. One of the most important tasks of criticism is to analyse the individuality of the artist (that is, his art) into its component elements, and to show their correlations. In this way, criticism brings the artist closer to the reader, who also has more or less of a "unique soul," artistically unexpressed, unchosen, but none the less representing a union of the same elements as does the soul of the poet. So it can be seen that what serves as a bridge from soul to soul is not the unique, but the common. Only through the common is the unique known; the common is determined in man by the deepest and most persistent conditions which make up his soul, by the social conditions of education, of existence, of work, and of association.[5]

What joins Manship and his works to his large and appreciative audience are the values they hold in common; they are conservative, and traditional. What he provides of the unique, while it is real and historically important, is a new subject matter made decorative — and palatable to the tastes of the Rockefellers, the Morgans, the Mellons, and to the official if synthetic personality of the United States government.

In 1920, when he was well into the successful twenty-five year period, his yearly income was estimated at sixty thousand dollars,[6] and he was described as one who "...dressed like the floor partner of a Stock Exchange house, and his clipped moustache, strong jaw, and somewhat imperative blue eyes recall the regular army officer rather than the sculptor."[7] Photographs of Manship taken throughout the course of his career invariably show him, if not in suit and tie, always in a dress shirt, high collar, tie, and proper artist's smock — even while at work in his studio.[8] This was no attempt to present himself as something he was not; rather, he appeared as what he was, an artist of the establishment. Reginald Marsh, only thirteen years Manship's junior, and working under what might be described as the grudgingly given patronage to the large group of artists who were still a minority, those within the Arts Project of the W.P.A., speaks of his own work on a mural in a Washington, D.C., post office. Certainly, it was not the right time for him.

Having mounted the scaffold without a colored smock and a tam-o-shanter resulted in many employees asking when the artist was coming along. This happened even after I had completed full length figures. In all the time I was there, no one asked me my name. ...Many wanted to know if there were new jobs in store for me and always looked at me in a pitying way. ...Most of them ventured that I must have been "born that way."[9]

23. *Eve*, 1925
gilded bronze, marble base
17 ⅜ x 5 ⅝ x 5 ⅝
66.14.66b
Murtha 185

24. *Icarus Falling,* 1965
gilded bronze and crystal quartz
10 x 6 x 5
66.14.30

These sculptures are part of a series of small works executed by Manship late in his career in which he used semi-precious quartz for the bases. The brilliance of the stones adds to the jewel-like quality of the works.

The two sculptures are similar. Both small simplified bodies retain only a hint of the archaic touch that Manship frequently employed, and both are executed on a spiral; Icarus on a vertical, Lucifer on a diagonal. Icarus is falling head-first toward the waves, his right wing melted and useless. Lucifer has fallen on his left shoulder and side, apparently unable to use his wings to arrest his descent.

According to myth, Icarus and his father Daedalus were imprisoned on the isle of Crete by King Minos. To escape, Daedalus fashioned two sets of wings from feathers and wax. He instructed his son that while flying, to follow a course midway between heaven and earth. After they had been flying for some time, Icarus began to enjoy the thrill of swooping and soaring through the air. He ignored his father's warning and flew too close to the sun. The heat melted the wax in his wings and Icarus fell to his death in the sea.

According to Christian belief, Lucifer was a proud, rebellious archangel, expelled from heaven, and thereafter known as Satan.
J.F.H.

If Manship were sensitive to what was right and proper in his time and place, and for whom, there were many like Marsh who were more sensitive, and, to their own detriment, to the deeper meanings of the same elements which Manship reflected in a more superficial and acceptable manner. These meanings had been introduced to the United States at the New York Armory Show of 1913. The manners of the responses of these artists, the degree of their sensitivity, had produced a disharmony between them and the public quite as potently destructive as the equally potent harmony between Manship and that same audience. The enmity of this public is echoed in an earlier letter by another artist, S. Macdonald-Wright (1890-1973):

For us there seems no kind of help or sympathy except the ridiculous plaudits of third-rate dilettantes and these only after we have suffered the rebuffs that no lackey even would put up with and have forced ourselves on a suspicious and uninterested public. By "us" I mean men who are seriously trying to push the boundaries of our art into realms yet untrod and who are really achieving something enroute. ...Why damnit it is a fact that artists, not merely painters, have no more esteemed place in their friends' and public's hearts than whores and that society treats both classes as pariahs with the obvious preference for the whores. (At least they travel in

25. *Lucifer*, 1956
gilded bronze and amethyst quartz, wood
base
7¾ x 7³/₁₆ x 4½
National Museum of American Art,
Smithsonian Institution
Gift of the Estate of Paul Manship
1966.47.61

automobiles and have charge accounts!)[10]

Some idea of the relative worths of the two groups of artists can be obtained by comparing Manship's constantly increasing income with the thirty-five dollars a week paid those on the W.P.A. projects; for example, in 1932, Manship received for a single commission, the Fort Wayne, Indiana, *Lincoln* (88), seventy-five thousand dollars.[11] The Federal government's attitude toward similar discrepancies, under the earlier administration of Herbert Hoover, had been referred to as a " 'trickle-down theory' " of economics and was described by its opponents as " 'feeding the sparrows by feeding the horses.' "[12] It was still being practiced. Manship was one of the lead-horses in the world of art. He was to sculpture what the successful entrepreneur was to commerce, and recognized as such. In the truest sense of the word, and for the time in question, Paul Manship defined the academician. He *was* the new academy.

What he does is derived in the fullest sense of the word. He has seen and studied with a passionate interest the work of sculptors of other ages, and from it {sic} has formed a powerful and intensely personal style which never diverges one inch from the standards set up by his predecessors. ...In a word, 'academic,' means simply the acceptance of certain conventions and techniques, certain methods of

26. *Orpheus,* 1927
bronze, marble base
9⅞ x 9¼ x 4
66.14.67a
Murtha 207

27. *Orpheus,* n.d.
pencil on paper
2¾ x 4¼
66.14.180 a

In the drawing, Orpheus is depicted as
inconsolable, mourning Eurydice. He is
shown holding his lyre in his left arm and
striking it with his right hand.

    The bronze sketch depicts Orpheus as
he begins his descent into Hades. He is
leaning forward on his left knee, striking
the lyre he holds above him. Manship
changed the position of the figure in the
drawing from one that is more horizontally
focused with a fluid, graceful line, to one
that is heavier and more earthbound for
the bronze sketch. Manship pursued this
subject again in a larger version in 1935.
(Murtha 352).
J.F.H.

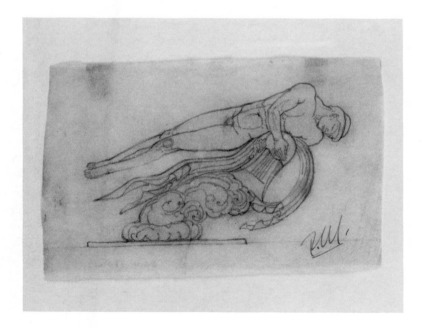

28. *Eurydice,* 1927
bronze, marble base
7¼ x 10 x 4⅜
66.14.67 b
Murtha 208

29. *Eurydice,* n.d.
pencil on papaer
3⅛ x 4½
66.14.180 b

In the drawing, Eurydice is depicted in Hades, lying in a stupor, her head pillowed on her right arm, her hair flowing freely. The figure is balanced on her right knee on the pointed rocks beneath her.

The bronze sketch depicts Eurydice in Hades unaware of the approach of Orpheus. She is in a swoon, reclining on her back on a rocklike base, her left arm circling her head.

The position of the figure in the bronze sketch is substantially altered from the drawing. In the drawing, Eurydice is transformed from a horizontal nude figure facing downward, to a draped, semi-reclining figure with her face upward. In 1935, Manship completed a larger version of Eurydice (Murtha 351 and 353).
J.F.H.

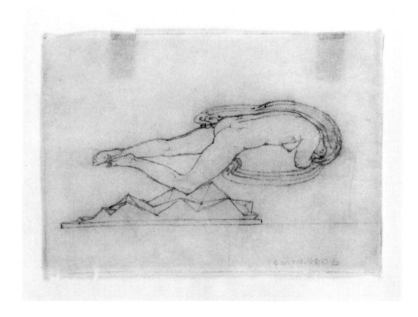

construction and systems of proportion which experience has shown to be
satisfactory.[13]

When the architects of the New York Rockefeller Center were asked why they had chosen Manship to make the fountain with its final figure of Prometheus, they answered:

Because Manship is the only man we can count on. ...We know that he'll turn out a 100% professional job, capably modeled, brilliantly cast, in scale, and with waterworks that work. And furthermore, on the opening day Manship will be there with the cord in his hand all ready to unveil.[14]

As Trotsky had pointed out, almost as if describing Manship's relationship to his patrons — architects as well as millionaires — the educational, social and associational conditions which had produced the sculptor had also produced his establishment audience. He was indeed the right man at the right time. He fit perfectly. He was not a "boundary-pusher;" his boundaries coincided with those of his patrons, within which both operated in complete freedom. Mr. Manship's work "...is implacably 'right,' so extraordinarily 'right' that sensitive and frail human beings get scared when they see it."[15] This fright was nothing less than the recognition of an absolute coincidence of viewer and artist; once that had been recognized, the valuation rested upon his craftsmanship. To blame the sculptor, in retrospect, for not assaulting the boundaries upon which he depended, is to ask that he be, have been, someone else.[16] At the time during which he was working within those limits, in complete freedom, a larger group, though still a minority by values displayed, saw those same limits as constraints. S. Macdonald-Wright was one, and there were many others in other fields: Sigmund Freud in Vienna; James Joyce in Trieste; Gertrude Stein, along with her *protégé* Ernest Hemingway, in Paris; and so was Albert Einstein in Berne. All of their boundary-pushing had been implicit, largely incipient in the United States, in the coming and going of the Armory Show. But this intellectual *avant-garde,* and its new set of values, remained a minority; its impact had been slight, certainly delayed, by the cultural inertia of a country which wanted " '...to turn backward and be safe. We wanted to mind our own business and to be left alone...' "[17]

To use Trotsky's term, the only unique thing about Manship's redefinition of the academic was the use of archaic subject matter and some of the *mudrās* of ancient India. He displayed these motifs in forms which were eminently acceptable to his patrons, to the older academicians, and even to many of the early moderns. His middle road, while not consciously selected as such, had appeared with perfect timing.

The first one-man exhibition of Mr. Manship's sculpture, which was held in New York late in the winter of 1916, created a veritable sensation among the larger public interested in artistic achievement. The extreme modernists and the academicians united in paying tribute to his genius; his success was complete.[18]

While there were some reservations about his work, its traditionally acceptable qualities were immediately recognized.

Mr. Manship's work is characterized by a perfection of craftsmanship. He lingers over his work with a loving hand, as did the designers of the coinage of ancient Greece, the makers of Limoges enamel and engraved crystal, as did Cellini when working with gold and enamel, as did the medalists of the Italian Renaissance. With a wealth of detail and a finish as exquisite as attained by the French eighteenth century maker of snuff-boxes, Mr. Manship's creations at the same time possess great simplicity and a perfect ensemble.[19]

The sculptor's *ensemble* was as polished and his position as secure as the values and wealth which supported it. The stock market crash of 1929 and the following depression had little effect on him. When many artists were signing pauper's certificates in order that they might work within the Public Works of Art Project of 1934, and then the W.P.A. of 1935, Manship had little need to concern himself. His later comments on the Project place him outside the involved group which included Reginald Marsh (1889-1954), Ben Shahn (1898-1969), John Flannagan (1895-1942), Louise Nevelson (1900-   ), Stuart Davis (1894-1964), and Jack Levine (1915-   ):

And for them {those who needed money to support themselves and their families} the W.P.A. was a fine thing, I think, at the time. And many works were done which otherwise would not have been done. They were not all masterpieces but there were some that were very fine. Well, one element that interested me, not that they were overly paid, because they were done as cheaply as possible, was the fact that many men who had been doing ivory tower art were brought out, and made to do decorations for public buildings, post offices; and what-not. And many painters who had only considered easel paintings done in their studios were asked to

30. *Orpheus*, 1950
bronze, marble base
10½ x 6⅞ x 3⅛
66.14.80

Orpheus is depicted with arms
outstretched, his lyre held in his left hand.
His head is tipped back and his mouth is
open as though singing.

Manship has streamlined and
simplified the figure. Orpheus is similar in
pose to *Prometheus Bringing Fire* (77)
executed the same year, but is more finely
modeled with careful attention to detail.
J.F.H.

*paint pictures that went on walls. They were subject to the sunshine of public
criticism which was a splendid thing. I have always contended that art must be
appreciated by the people, and when art becomes too much of a game between the
artist and his small group of sympathizers — or big, as the case may be — it isn't
complete. Who was it said that art, to be truly great must be the art of the common
people, who understand and appreciate it?*[20]

While Manship's criticism of many of the modernists was more gentle
than that of others, including his patrons, it was based upon precisely the
same set of criteria.

I must say that the impressionistic abstractions of some sculptors today are not sympathetic to me because some willful distortion of nature today is, I think, unfortunate. Nature is so marvelous and so beautiful, glorious and so little attainable, after all. ...The individualized exaggeration of today little conforms to, or is in sympathy with, the artists' attitude which was common in the Gothic period.[21]

His subject matter was most frequently drawn from the same sources which were influential among the modernists, but his forms were those of the Renaissance masters tempered by accepted standards and conditioned by modern technology.

When an artist employs an archaic or a primitive motif, he may do so in two ways. In the first, which is Manship's way, he presents a subject-matter from a distant time and/or place in a form which is that of his time and place. In a sense, what he offers is a quotation from the past, or the distant time, or both. If that foreign work of art engenders a deeply felt response, another artist may "use" it in an entirely different way. In this instance its form will not likely resemble the foreign work at all, but present a meaning which will be analogous to the meaning of the original. Of such works one is inclined to say, "They transcend time itself, present timeless values." While this is indeed an overstatement, it does help characterize the difference between a topical work and one that endures.[22] Manship's sculpture was a streamlining of archaic motifs in accordance with the taste of his time, and of his patrons.

At first the moderns tended to see him as one of their own, a herald of what he later called "willful distortions of nature." The academicians saw him as a continuation of proper traditions. "Manship stands practically alone in sculptural technique. His works defy imitation as do those of Benvenuto Cellini. They are supreme."[23] Cellini, like Manship, worked for the *cognoscenti* of his time, including Popes, Cardinals, the Medici of Florence, and Francis I, King of France. In retrospect, the American's Cellinesque supremacy was entirely predictable. His subject matter was archaic, thus participating in the newly aroused concern for the primitive; his forms were those of tradition; and his finish that of the late Renaissance and eighteenth century snuff boxes. His castings were done in the best foundries, that second oldest profession, and his technology was that of the epitome of industry, the automobile. In 1933, his career was

31. *Orpheus Playing the Lyre to Pegasus,* n.d.
ink and pencil on paper
6½ x 11¾
66.14.145a.

Pegasus is shown flying above the clouds
with Orpheus' image superimposed in
front of him. Manship combines the image
of Orpheus, the musician, with that of
Pegasus and his association with poetic
inspiration.

   Orpheus was the son of Apollo and
Calliope, the Muse of Epic Poetry. He had
a magic lyre, made by Hermes, which he
was taught to play with such perfection
that none could resist its spell. He
charmed trees and rivers as well as animals
of the wild and mankind.

   According to myth, the winged horse
Pegasus sprang from the blood of Medusa
when Perseus cut off her head. Soon after
birth, Pegasus flew to Mount Helicon
where he opened the Hippocrene fountain
with a kick of his hoof. Whoever drank
from this fountain received the gift of song
and of poetic inspiration. Pegasus became
the favorite of the nine Muses and was
always at the service of poets.

   The drawing with its defined border is
similar to one of three relief panels on the
facade of the Norton Gallery & School of
Art, entitled *Inspiration.* Both the drawing
and panel show Orpheus playing the lyre,
superimposed against Pegasus flying in the
clouds, and are similar in their rectangular
shapes, completely filling the horizontal
space.
J.F.H.

32. *Orpheus with Pegasus,* n.d.
black chalk and pencil on paper
14¹¹/₁₆ x 18¼
National Museum of American Art,
Smithsonian Institution
Gift of the Estate of Paul Manship
1966.47.209

Orpheus and Pegasus are positioned
differently in this drawing. The body of
the horse and its wings are cropped, the
diagonal is emphasized, resulting in a
somewhat awkward pose for Orpheus.
Orpheus is depicted holding the large lyre
in his lap with his left hand, striking it
with his right. Pegasus rears and paws the
air behind him, anxious to be off.

MMA owns a similar chalk drawing of
Orpheus and Pegasus in which Manship
employed the device of cutting off the
figures at the edges of the page
(66.14.150).
J.F.H.

described as marching along

> *gaining cumulative force as though it were a thing in nature — as indeed I
> begin to suspect it is — and now he has reached the point when he is acknowledged
> to be the most successful sculptor in the country — the sculptor to whom all the
> important jobs naturally gravitate.*[24]

Manship's *entrée* to what was to remain a charmed circle for more than
twenty-five years began with his winning the Prix de Rome in 1909. His
exhibition debut was made at the Architectural League of New York in
1912 where he

> *sold so many bronzes, at prices ranging from five hundred to a thousand
> dollars apiece, that at twenty-seven he found himself suddenly quite well off. He
> had found his market and it has, since then, wonderfully increased.*[25]

This statement would summarize his standing in the eyes of the
nation, by his own judgment, until the Second World War. In 1943, he
had been the subject of some complimentary remarks made to the Board of
Directors of the Indianapolis Museum of Art by Booth Tarkington. The
latter had heard Manship speak there in April of that year and had
identified himself as a stalwart, if older, admirer. Manship wrote the
author to thank him for his praise: "And as to the *boost.* It is wonderful,
and will undoubtedly lead lots of people to believe that I am quite a guy
— which I desire as I am always fearful that the old reputation will
slump."[26] On the fifteenth of May, the sculptor received the following
reply:

> *"Always fearful that the old reputation will slump," you say, and upon that I
> wish you could have a talk, some time, with one of the refugees referred to above —
> Dr. Erwin Panofsky now of the Princeton Institute like Einstein his friend.
> Panofsky's tracing of the periods of great artists is illuminating, and, if I rightly
> recall his idea*[27]*, it is that the final (usually the third) period is the most
> interesting to the minds of intelligent observers. I suppose this is as much as to say
> that in a completed maturity an artist may "lose his public" but will retain the
> Best Few. Sometimes he has both. So far as such a recluse as I can know, you have
> both. "Commercially" the way of the sculpture {sic} and painter can't now be
> enlivened by "private collectors." Taxes and the advance of State Socialism have
> pretty well wiped out that unfortunate feller — he doesn't control enough votes to
> save himself. After the war, however, the sculptor should "come back," Monuments
> and Memorials. Of course it's true that under Socialism (i.e. Politicians) many of*

33. *Pegasus*, 1937
bronze, marble base
6¾ x 6⅛ x 3
66.14.85
Murtha 372

These small *Pegasus* sculptures are studies for memorial tablet finials. The 1937 study was executed for the *Rufus Lenoir Patterson 3rd Memorial*, 1945 (Murtha 454), and the 1943 study for the *Otis Skinner Memorial*, 1943 (Murtha 439).

In the 1937 *Pegasus*, the fabled winged horse is caught in a pensive mood. His head is down, and his motionless body, cradled gently by a billowing cloud, is apparently at rest. In the later study, however, *Pegasus* surges upward, is poised for flight, his muzzle pointed skyward, readying himself to soar through the heavens in search of adventure.

The sixth century mythographer Fulgentius described Pegasus as a symbol of Fame, since he is winged, as was the traditional depiction of Fame.* Pegasus also is a heroic figure, since his riders, Bellerophon and Perseus, were able to conquer their enemies while mounted upon the winged horse's back. This identification with Fame and heroic deeds makes him an appropriate subject for a memorial tablet. The symbolism of Pegasus as a cloud dweller also suggests the promise of immortality for the individuals commemorated by the tablets.
*James Hall, *Dictionary of Subjects & Symbols in Art* (New York: Harper & Row, Publishers, Inc., 1979), 238.
L.A.K.
S.L.

the commissions go to the wrong people — somebody's brother-in-law — but you're undoubtedly the "most famous" American Sculptor, your name has gone over the land for years and carries more weight than any other. People used to know about St. Gaudens and French, now they very generally know only about you. That isn't wiped out so quickly.[28]

In this exchange of letters, there is tacit acknowledgment that Manship's qualifications as the "right man" were indeed in question, if only because the "right time" had passed. Tarkington's insistence upon the arrival of "Socialism" as a primary determinant of the slump was an indirect observation that the values which had sustained the artist had been obliterated. The trauma of the Second World War had raised questions which could no longer be answered by reference to old values; these questions were being answered by a new set, those of the non-isolationist moderns who were no longer a minority.

The voice of the new had been applied to Manship's work at least as early as 1920, though it was heard by few outside its own meager circle.

34. *Pegasus,* 1943
terra-cotta relief
9¾ x 9 x 1¾
Collection Mr. and Mrs.
Thomond R. O'Brien
Murtha 437

e.e. cummings, writing in *The Dial* of that year, had reviewed the work of one of Manship's assistants on the J.P. Morgan Memorial (Fig. 3) for the Metropolitan Museum, Gaston Lachaise. In doing so, he made scathing reference to the sculpture of the master:

One wonders whether his winning the Prix de Rome accounts for the fact that in the last analysis Manship is neither a sincere alternative to thinking, nor an appeal to the pure intelligence, but a very ingenious titillation of that well-known element, the highly sophisticated unintelligence. ...Fundamentally Manship is one of those producers of "modern statues" ...His work is, of course, superior to the masterpieces of such people as French, Barnard, Bartlett, the Borglums, and Bela Pratt — in so far as something which is thoroughly dead is superior to something which has never been alive.[29]

If one removes cummings' delightfully witty venom, it appears that he saw early and clearly the flaws which would eventually lead to Manship's slump, his fall from gracious appreciation. In the first place, he describes the artist's work as "thoroughly dead," that is, drawn from an antiquity

35. *Pegasus,* n.d.
ink wash over pencil on cardboard
8 x 6
66.14.145 c

In this ink wash, a heavier, bolder style is
employed. Pegasus rears above a lyre, his
wings flared with his head thrown back
and mouth partially open. Despite the
freer, looser style, Pegasus remains a
beautifully-proportioned animal.
J.F.H.

which had once been alive. They were seen as lifeless reconstructions of
archaic forms in modern dress. Second, they offered nothing new and were
therefore easily acceptable. And third, he chooses to identify Manship's
patronage as that larger group of the American public who possessed a
"highly sophisticated unintelligence," — and a not inconsiderable wealth.
cummings' criticism is very close to that which might describe the
sculptor's works as a series of quotations which were inappropriate despite
the vernacular in which they were delivered. Manship's archaisms were

54

dead, if charmingly so. The moderns would draw upon the same sources, but would accomplish a true resurrection — either as an appeal to the pure intelligence in the forms of Cubism and its derivatives, or as sincere alternatives to thinking in the forms of Expressionism.

When the fall occurred it was abrupt. Emily Genauer, writing in the December 1951 *New York Herald-Tribune* of the American Sculpture Exhibition at the Metropolitan Museum provides an evaluation which had been current for some time:

If the works on display reveal little originality of form they indicate even less imagination in concept. Our sculptors, for all their technical facility, have apparently little to say.[30]

She then singles out Manship's memorial for the American cemetery at Anzio. *It's so bad it's downright embarrassing. It depicts two barechested American doughboys {sic}, as expressionless and about as sculptural as a pair of department store dummies.*[31]

A.L. Chanin, writing in the *Compass* comments similarly: *two placid, photographic figures, smooth and pretty, complete from dog tags to carefully delineated belt-buckles and shoe laces...*[32]

which he also compared to the Bond Store figures on New York's Times Square. Howard Devree, writing in *The New York Times*, saw Manship's figures as related to "the monstrous figures in that clothing advertisement display on Times Square."[33] By 1957, when George McCue reviewed Edwin Murtha's lavishly illustrated book on the sculptor, even the weak appreciation of technical facility had disappeared.

to survey...{a great many of Manship's works at one time} is to experience a haunting conviction that in his prodigiously productive lifetime, Manship has set sculpture as an art form, back approximately 2000 years. {His works}...have a way of looking like the ornaments that used to adorn automobile radiator caps.[34]

As the right man at the right time, Paul H. Manship was supremely successful, certainly by the standards of the prevailing majority. When those standards failed, when the old values no longer applied, the time had passed and he was no longer the right man.[35]

Dr. Frederick D. Leach
Hamline University

Notes

1
Henry McBride, quoted by Rosamund Frost, "Manship Ahoy," *Art News* 44 (June 1945): 28. Miss Frost does not cite her source.

2
Paul H. Manship, to Paul K. Manship, 1952. Paul K. Manship, interview by Frederick D. Leach, Mahtomedi, Minnesota, March 1972.

3
Paul H. Manship, interview by John D. Morse, 18 February 1950, transcript, 11, *Archives of American Art,*

4
Royal Cortissoz, *New York Herald-Tribune,* 15 April 1933.

5
Leon Trotsky, *Literature and Revolution,* trans. Rose Strunsky (London: Allen and Unwin, 1925), 59-60. Italics mine. For a detailed analysis of these concepts see: Erwin Panofsky, "Introductory," in *Studies in Iconology* (New York: Oxford University Press, 1939), 3-31.

6
Cameron Rogers, "Profiles: The Compleat Sculptor," *The New Yorker Magazine,* 4 (1 September 1928): 23.

7
Rogers, "Profiles," 23.

8
Frederick D. Leach, *Paul Howard Manship: An Intimate View* (Saint Paul: Minnesota Museum of Art, 1972), passim.

9
Reginald Marsh, *The Artist in America* (New York: W.W. Norton Co., Inc., 1967), 175. Statement dated 1935.

10
S. Macdonald-Wright, *The Artist in America* (New York: W.W. Norton Co., Inc., 1967), 157. Statement dated 1917.

11
George Biddle, *The Artist in America* (New York: W.W. Norton Co., Inc., 1967), 174. Biddle's statement regarding the weekly wage of the WPA employee is dated 11 December 1933. Manship's commission for the Fort Wayne *Lincoln* is taken from the Morse interview, transcript, 23, *Archives of American Art.*

12
"The Depression Years," in William J. Chute, ed., *The American Scene: 1860 to the Present,* 2 (New York: Bantam Books, 1966), 340.

13
Stanley Casson, *Twentieth Century Sculptors* (London: Oxford University Press, 1930), 42-43.

14
Article, Rosamund Frost, the renovation of Manship's work on the sculpture of the Rockefeller Center, *New York Times,* 8 April 1984.

15
Cortissoz, *New York Herald-Tribune,* 15 April 1933.

16
All artists necessarily reflect their times, and places; this cannot be otherwise. That some may speak clearly to other times and places is not to say they are not of their times. Trotsky's comments are *apropos,* as are those of Henri Matisse: "Whether we like it or not, and however insistently we may call ourselves exiles, there is an indissoluble bond between our period and

ourselves." Pierre Schneider, *Matisse*, trans. Michael Taylor and Bridget Stevens Romer (New York: Rizzoli, 1984) and *New York Times Book Review*, 25 November 1984.

17
William L. Chenery, *So It Seemed* (New York: Harcourt Brace Jovanovich, 1952), 133.

18
Albert E. Gallatin, *Paul Manship: A Critical Essay on His Sculpture and on Iconography* (New York: John Lane, 1917), 1.

19
Gallatin, *Paul Manship*, 8-9.

20
Morse interview, transcript, 12. *Archives of American Art*. Morse answered Manship's question, "Tolstoy."

21
Morse interview, transcript, 21. *Archives of American Art*.

22
Dr. Erwin Panofsky deals with analogous shifts of form and content in his "Renaissance and Renascences," *Kenyon Review* (Spring 1944): 201-235. On the imitation of the antique, cf. Edward Young, "Conjectures on Original Composition," (1759), in Mark Schorer, Josephine Miles, and Gordon McKenzie, eds., *Criticism: The Foundations of Modern Literary Judgment* (New York: Harcourt Brace Jovanovich, 1948), 12-30, esp. 15.

That the sculptor did look upon the past as an encyclopedic collection of motifs from which he could select "quotations" is indicated when he remarked: "Each generation, I'm sure, looks upon classic antiquity with new eyes. I was more interested in the older styles of the ancients. Whereas a man like French was involved with the highly developed and mature work of the classical periods. …You'll find that each decade goes farther back into the primitive and in the studies of primitive art. With the result that now it is gone practically as far as it can with the art of the Cyclades, the art of the Negro, the primitive art of the Pacific islands, too. So that we have gained and gone the full turn to the beginning." Morse interview, transcript, 7, *Archives of American Art*.

23
Frank O. Payne, "Two Amazing Portraits by Paul Manship," *International Studies*, 71 (October 1920): 24.

24
Cortissoz, *New York Herald-Tribune*, 15 April 1933.

25
Rogers, "Profiles," 22.

26
NY 59-16, *Archives of American Art*.

27
Tarkington recalls Panofsky's idea, but in comforting his friend he misconstrues it.

28
NY 59-17, *Archives of American Art*.

29
e.e. cummings, "Gaston Lachaise," *Dial* 68 (January-June 1920): 194-95.

30
Emily Genauer, *New York Herald-Tribune*, quoted in "Sad, Sad Commentary," *Art Digest* 26 (1 January 1952): 11. The specific source is not cited, nor is the December 1951 date.

31
"Sad, Sad Commentary."

32
"Sad, Sad Commentary".

33
"Sad, Sad Commentary."

34
George McCue, *St. Louis Post-Dispatch*, 28 April 1957. McCue must have had the Rockefeller *Prometheus* in mind.

35
After completing this essay, my attention was drawn by Prof. James Conaway, Hamline University, to a very perceptive and informative article by Susan Rather, "The Past Made Modern: Archaism in American Sculpture," *Arts Magazine*, (November 1984), 111-20. Miss Rather's precise and discriminating differentiation between primitivism and archaism is enlightening.

(see frontispiece)
36. *Fame,* 1926
pink Georgia marble
26 x 28 x 4½
66.14.101
Murtha 196

Following his own dictum, "art follows war," Manship received many commissions for peace and war memorials. The angel, *Fame,* is carved in high relief and shows Manship's Art Deco style at its zenith. The streamlined figure moves swiftly to the left, her head turned sharply back over her shoulder. Her long horn runs parallel with her extended arm, stabilizing the composition. Manship's handling of the square space with a subject that extends beyond the confines of the border, recalls the sculptural metopes of the Parthenon with their active scenes. Often the head turning back over the shoulder was the Greek artist's resolution of the border restriction. Here, *Fame's* wing extends from the edges on three sides, as well as her foot on the right, adding a sense of energy and movement to the work.

Completed in limestone for the *Soldier's Monument* in the American Cemetery at Thiaucourt, France, the memorial is in the shape of a Latin Cross. *Fame* is set in an upper recess, a full-size figure of a soldier placed below. This delicate pink marble version is the only full-size replica completed in preparation for the final work.

The personification of *Fame* as a female figure was known in classical antiquity, and is often found in the company of the illustrious dead, whom she carries away on wings that never tire, according to

Horace.* Her trumpet was introduced in the Renaissance; she is usually found in association with historical figures, and seen on funerary sculpture.
*Horace, *Odes,* bk. 2, sec. 2, 7-8; cited in James Hall, *Dictionary of Subjects and Symbols in Art* (New York: Harper & Row, Publishers, Inc., 1979), 119.
G.K.

Fig. 4
Soldiers Monument, 1926, American Cemetery, Thiaucourt, France limestone, life-size figure

37. *Study for Portal of Freedom*, n.d.
ink on paper
7 x 4⅞
66.14.186

38. *Portal of Freedom Sketch*, 1941
bronze, marble base
18⅛ x 6½ x 6
66.14.68
Murtha 423

The drawing for the bronze sketch shows the torch being carried in the figure's left hand. The figure of the man appears larger, more heavily muscled in the drawing than when realized in the bronze sketch. In the bronze, the primary figure holds a torch aloft in his right hand, while clustered behind him are subsidiary figures that represent Labor, Science, Arts and Letters, Design, Constructions, etc. Justice is conventionally represented, a blindfolded woman holding scales in one of her hands, on the sides of the pedestal.

Manship, working in collaboration with architect Jacques Carlu, made this bronze sketch for a proposed monument, never realized.
J.F.H.

39. *Aviation Memorial Sketch,* 1939
bronze, wood base
20⅜ x 8½ x 4
66.14.18
Murtha 394

In 1939 Manship was commissioned by
the Aero Club in Philadelphia to execute a
memorial for the aviators who died in
World War I. The *Aviation Memorial Sketch*
may have been a preliminary study for the
monument.

This bronze study is mounted on a tall
wooden structure supported at the bottom
by two stylized trapezoidal steps. A nude
male figure in a posture suggesting flight
is placed diagonally within a half-circle
ring. World War I vintage biplanes fly
amid clouds at the man's feet. In 1944, a
celestial sphere was chosen as the subject
for the *Aero Memorial.*
S.L.

Paul Manship and the Genesis of Archaism

40. *Dancer and Gazelles,* 1916
bronze
32½ x 33 x 10
1966.47.8
National Museum of American Art,
Smithsonian Institution
Gift of the Estate of Paul Manship
Murtha 85

The essence of East Indian art is captured
in the graceful, rhythmic movement of the
dancer centered between two gazelles.
Most striking is the frontal quality of the
work, with emphasis on the silhouette.
The animals which flank the central figure
are simplified and sleek, which further
heightens decorative folds and border
designs on the garment of the dancer.

It appears as if the woman is
communicating with the animals; to the
animal on the left who is jumping up we
see her giving a "stay" command; on the
right she appears to be holding a morsel or
signaling to the animal who is about to
leap.

The *contrapposto* stance of the dancer is
reminiscent of classical Greek art and the
tortion of her body is a gesture Manship
derived from Indian art. The heraldic
design of the entire composition evokes
Minoan, Mycenean, as well as
Mesopotamian sources, where animals
often flank a sacred personnage, column or
central figure.

Manship was awarded the Helen Foster
Barnett Prize at the National Academy of
Design, New York, for the lifesize version
of *Dancer and Gazelles* in 1917.
J.H.
G.K.

Paul Manship's career began in earnest in 1905, when he left his native
Saint Paul to study in the East. He was first briefly enrolled at the Art
Students League of New York and later studied with Charles Grafly at the
Pennsylvania Academy of the Fine Arts (1907-1908).[1] Both by his choice
of schools and the limited time spent in them, Manship largely avoided a
traditional artistic education, based on such academically-sanctioned
models as classical and Hellenistic Greek sculpture. This may well have
contributed to the lack of prejudice with which he subsequently
approached the hitherto largely ignored arts of pre-classical Greece, early
medieval Europe, and the Far East — from which the stylistic elements of
early twentieth-century archaism were derived.

In learning his craft, Manship considered the periods he spent in
apprenticeship to sculptors Solon Borglum (1905-1907) and Isidore Konti
(1908-1909) to have been more instructive than art school. Under their
careful tutelage, he advanced from near ignorance about the practice of
sculpture to a state of tolerable accomplishment. Following the example of
his teachers, naturalism — in style and subject matter — characterizes
Manship's early work, as may be seen in his *End of Day,* 1909.

The most significant factor in the development of Manship's archaism
was the period he spent as a fellow at the American Academy in Rome
(1909-1912). For an artist of Manship's generation, Rome was an unusual
destination and he even once admitted "no particular desire to go to
Rome, having always looked upon Paris as the art Mecca."[2] "There is not a
thought-wave in modern art that does not emanate from or finally reach
Paris," wrote critic Charles Caffin; "It is the world's clearing-house of
artistic currency."[3] For the young artist, a sojourn in that city was
considered essential, and to go to Rome was to condemn oneself to an
artistic backwater. One artist even intoned, with specific reference to the
American Academy: "I pity any artist doomed to Rome for three years.
Art is certainly dead there and you might as well bury him as to let him
go to Rome."[4]

Initially, it might seem strange that Rome was the location chosen for
an American academy by its founders, since most of them had, in fact,
studied in Paris. Indeed, Paris offered a superb educational system, but to
the cultural elite of late nineteenth-century America, it was lacking in

Fig. 5
Centaur and Nymph Dancing, 1910
(destroyed)

Fig. 6
Duck Girl, 1911

classical grandeur. Even the French seemed to acknowledge this by awarding their finest students a four-year Prix de Rome.[5] Even so, the American Academy's founders had a problem: "We need to inculcate the love for Italy," one bluntly stated; "Paris is the loadstone that attracts."[6]

Part of the problem in maintaining a hold on the fellows was a lack of clear structure at the Academy. As explained by its director:

The Academy has no staff of instructors and does not aim to teach technique, methods or processes. The course of study at the Academy is one of observation and research more than of original design. The aim is to form a correct taste and to impress upon the mind, by daily contact with great examples, those fundamental principles that are essential to enduring quality in art, be the style what it may.[7]

Fellows were thus assumed to be advanced students who required only a period of immersion in the tradition-steeped environment of Rome to ensure their future as apostles of culture in America. However, this goal simply did not translate into a specific and easily followed procedure.

Most of Manship's predecessors at the Academy had sorely disappointed its officers because they seemed so oblivious to their environment. As the institution's secretary lamented: "no one really takes advantage of their {sic} surroundings. They sit in bare studios and try to be original!! Wow! it makes me sick."[8] Manship would prove the exception to this pattern, and the trustees' delight is clearly registered in the comment of one "that this man alone may be worth to American Art all the effort the American Academy in Rome has cost."[9] However, in view of the Academy's lack of success in forcing enlightenment on the fellows, it must be underscored that Manship's receptivity to the art of the past — and to archaic Greek art, most significantly — arose out of his own curiosity. By granting him a fellowship, the Academy placed Manship in the position to develop as an artist, but it did not offer him specific training in an archaistic (or any other) style.

The process whereby Manship arrived at his archaism may be traced in his annual Academy projects. In the first year, he created a life-size relief of a centaur and nymph dancing, known only through a photograph (Fig. 5). Its exuberant mood, plastic composition, and theme immediately evoke the joyous bacchanals of the eighteenth-century French sculptor Clodion, and find more immediate precedent in the Viennese neo-baroque style

41. *Vase*, 1913
bronze
14⅝ x 8½ x 5¼
Collection Corcoran Gallery of Art,
Washington, D.C.
Bequest of James Parmelee, 1941
41.72
Murtha 32

According to Vitry, Manship made this vase for his wife. This is one of the few small vases that he made; large-scale vases for gardens characterize his work in this genre.

The art historical prototype for the body of this vase is the classical Greek amphora. The curvilinear ornament and the griffin-head handles, however, are Far Eastern in style, similar to those found on a distinctive type of bronze vessel cast by Greek artists of the late seventh century B.C. John Boardman describes the griffin ornament in the following manner:

*The motif is Eastern but the treatment is Greek, and Greek artists soon elaborate the monstrous high ears, forehead knob, gaping beak and sinuous neck into an entirely new decorative form.**

The female dancer that adorns the front of the vessel resembles Manship's *Salome* (43). The source of inspiration for both figures appears to have been the "apsaras," or celestial females, as seen in the art of India. These voluptuous women were generally depicted swaying in the highly exaggerated yet elegant movements of East Indian dance.

*John Boardman, *Greek Art* (New York: Praeger Publishers, 1964), 37.
L.A.K.
S.L.

practiced by Manship's last teacher, Isidore Konti. The relief does not, then, derive inspiration from archaic (or even classical) sculpture; however, it represents a significant break from Manship's more prosaic early themes and inaugurates his love affair with playful subjects from pagan antiquity.

The second year's sculpture was the life-size *Duck Girl* (Fig. 6). Already, in this piece, we sense the vigor of Manship's early mature style and the reasons for his success; in the words of one critic: "He displays a peculiar gift for the fusion of a modern naturalism with an antique distinction of style."[10] Kenyon Cox, the academic painter and art critic,

Fig. 7
Greek bronze, *"Narcissus."* Naples, Museo Nazionale

Fig. 8
The Mask of Silenus, 1912 (destroyed).

was similarly struck. If the *Duck Girl* reminded him of "the best Pompeian bronzes," he also felt himself strongly in the presence of a "precocious Italian girl of to-day," and he concluded that with this piece: "We are as far from the mechanically constructed pseudo-classic ideal as from vulgar realism...It seems to me an original work of true classic inspiration."[11]

In fact, a specific antique source for the *Duck Girl* can be identified in an elegant bronze sculpture of a youth from Pompeii, now in Naples (Fig. 7). By virtue of this ancient source alone, the *Duck Girl* moves us closer to Manship's archaistic style. However, it is worth noting that the source of inspiration is Hellenistic — a relatively "baroque" phase of ancient sculpture — and, thus, a logical step from Manship's first-year work, with its neo-baroque antecedents.

Manship's principal project during his final year at the Academy was an heroic-sized sculpture of a man with a grotesque mask teasing a child, which lends the work its title — *The Mask of Silenus* (Fig. 8). Here again, the motif evokes Hellenistic sculpture, most notably the well-known *Hermes with the Infant Dionysus,* by Praxiteles. However, the mask is decidedly archaic in inspiration, and may have been based on a late sixth-century antefix.[12] This appropriation from archaic art, especially from its more decorative forms, marks the beginning of Manship's archaism, a style he would soon realize more successfully in statuette form. Indeed, one might say that his particular talent for creating playful and decorative statuettes was unleashed by his exposure to pre-classical Greek art. This, at any rate, was the opinion of Manship's dealer, Martin Birnbaum, who later concluded that Manship

found himself only after he began to appreciate the Greek primitives...those minute fragments which reveal the simpler and lighter phases of the classic spirit. A little head spouting water, an intense painting on a vase, a carved intaglio, a precious coin, the exquisite bronze claw of the statuette of some animal, — these humbler forms helped him to analyze the nobler secrets of the ancients.[13]

The catalyst for Manship's archaism was the trip he made to Greece in the spring of 1912. He was evidently predisposed to appreciate archaic work, having written Konti prior to this trip: "I am at present quite crazy about the Early Greek Art and expect to draw everything that I can lay my eyes upon."[14] Unfortunately, only a few of his Greek drawings remain,

Fig. 9
Kore, c. 500 B.C., Athens, Acropolis
Museum.

including full-size studies of details from the Parthenon and Erectheum in Athens, and the Treasury of the Siphnians at Delphi (47).

Most of all, in Greece, Manship was taken with archaic and severe-style sculpture, and with vase painting, which he found "to be directly relevant of [sic] Greek sculpture."[15] He very much admired the Charioteer of Delphi — "the finest extant example of bronze sculpture" — and the archaic korai excavated from the Athenian Acropolis in the 1880s (e.g. Fig. 9).[16] In a lecture at the Academy, after his return from Greece, he assessed their appeal as follows:

we feel the power of design, the feeling for structure in line, the harmony in the divisions of spaces and masses — the simplicity of the flesh admirably contrasted by rich drapery, every line of which is drawn with precision. It is the decorative value of the line that is considered first. Nature is formalized to conform with the artist's idea of beauty. Just as the sculptor in modelling foliated forms to be used in architectural decoration reduced nature to its decorative essence and considered the relationship of lines and masses rather than reality, so in these statues the artist has subordinated everything to his formal composition. The entire statue can be considered as a decorative form upon which all the detail is drawn rather than modelled.[17]

These words are among Manship's most famous, for not only do they astutely describe the characteristics and appeal of Greek archaic work, but also of Manship's own, as it would develop in the wake of this experience. Thus, the trip to Greece, during which he discovered archaic art, was the turning point for Manship. "He who loves beauty for beauty's sake," he would later say, "will ever go back to those early works of the primitives."[18] Manship did exactly that, and the study of these "primitives" formed the basis of his archaistic style.

Manship made his professional debut as an artist in February 1913, at the Architectural League's annual exhibition in New York. This event, which brought him immediate critical and popular acclaim, marks the beginning of a long and successful career. Although Manship is today thoroughly identified with the academic cause (as he would wish to be), it is important to note that initially, at least, he exerted a much broader appeal. Indeed, in considering the critical response to Manship's showing at the League, one is struck by the fact of his acceptance by both

Fig. 10
Scene from *L'Après-midi d'un Faun*

conservative and more liberal critics.

The arch-academic Kenyon Cox, for example, found Manship's archaistic statuettes, such as the *Lyric Muse* (9) or the *Centaur and Dryad* (42), to be "almost uniformly successful and charming." Quite in spite of their archaizing details, they were "full of the direct observation of life and of an essential modernity." As Cox observed, "to see this archaistic manner applied to figures with a quite unarchaic freedom of movement, doing things that no archaic sculptor would have thought of making them do, is oddly exhilarating."[19]

In developing a style that borrowed from archaic Greece, Manship did nothing overtly unacceptable to his mentors, because he was not repudiating the past — although the aesthetic of archaism had not previously been a part of the working academic vocabulary. Still, however little his sculptures conformed in some aspects to established and idealized types, they were undeniably based on a thorough knowledge of antique styles and subjects — and no models were more revered by the academic community. Academics also recognized in Manship a guardian of time-honored traditions of craftsmanship, which seemed to them to be ignored by many modernists. Indeed, modernism (however one chose to define it) and careful craftsmanship were so widely regarded by academics as mutually exclusive that their coincidence in Manship's sculptures — "extremely 'modern,' and yet thoroughly workmanlike" — seemed promising indeed.[20]

That Manship's works could be perceived more as modernist experiments than academic repetitions is further suggested by the criticism of Charles Caffin. In particular, he was struck by Manship's handling of the heads and draperies in the *Centaur and Dryad* (42), and offered them as evidence that the artist was "searching after a more abstract treatment of form."[21] Significantly, then, it was the archaic-inspired details (although they are not identified using that term) that caught Caffin's attention, along with the work's emotional expressiveness. These factors caused him tentatively to rank Manship among the country's promising young modernists.

Within a few years of his New York debut, Manship had attained considerable fame. In spite of periodic doubts raised by art critics, his

42. *Centaur and Dryad*, 1913
bronze
27⅜ x 18⅜ x 11⁷⁄₁₆
Smith College Museum of Art,
Northampton, Massachusetts,
Purchased 1915
Murtha 28

Centaur and Dryad was recognized as one of Manship's finest works, and was awarded the Helen Foster Barnett prize at New York's National Academy of Design shortly after it was completed in 1913, and its early purchase by The Metropolitan Museum of Art in 1914 further enhanced Manship's growing reputation.

Greek archaism is a predominant theme in the work: in the sensually portrayed subject of the centaur pursuing the beautiful but protesting nymph, in the execution of the stiff stylization of the hair and beard, and angular stylized drapery windswept to the right to spatially resolve an otherwise awkward gap. The silhouette forms are crisply delineated and recall incised black figure painting.

The base is an important part of the work, and Manship always had a special concern for this aspect of his sculpture. In this work, it is almost as important as the object itself and sets the stage for the scene. Griffins decorate the sides of the base; scenes of revelry are carved in relief on the front and back. The lower part of the base features tigers, lions, foxes, rabbits, alluding to Manship's continual love for animal themes.
G.K.

archaistic sculptures continued to appeal and enchant, and no wonder: Manship was a consummate designer and craftsman, and this, combined with charmingly uncomplicated subjects, conveyed an aura of disarming sophistication. It was during this period of the mid-teens that his archaism reached its fullest development.

To the importance of early Greek art in Manship's aesthetic, another element was added at this time — the influence of India. "We can no longer hide behind the Elgin marbles and refuse to look" at non-Western art, the vanguard English critic Roger Fry had commented in 1910, at a time when Indian art had just begun to attract serious attention.[22] His message was directed especially at artists, for whom he felt the study of Eastern art would be positive and liberating. It is a mark of this period that interest in the art of non-Western cultures was so often inseparable from concern for its applicability to contemporary artistic developments. The "primitive" arts (including the archaic) emerged from the province of archaeologists to assume simultaneous importance to art historians and artists. In this context, Manship's receptivity to such art must be considered advanced.

43. *Salome*, 1915
bronze
19½ x 13⅜ x 10½
66.14.27
Murtha 73

In the New Testament account of Saint
John the Baptist, Salome, the daughter of
Herodias, danced at King Herod's
birthday celebration, and so pleased him
that he swore on oath he would give her
whatever she asked of him.

    At her mother's behest, Salome asked
for the head of John the Baptist on a plate.
Herod had imprisoned John for publicly
speaking against his liaison with Herodias,
the wife of his brother Philip. Herod
upheld his oath, and had John executed.
Salome accepted the grisly prize, and gave
it to her vengeful mother.

    Given the repellent theme, there is
remarkably little emotional content in the
work. In dying so valiantly not one
carefully-tended archaic curl is in disarray.
Salome's drooping head and parted lips
may connote a modicum of sorrow, but
may also suggest the depth of her
involvement in the dance. Manship's
penchant for a decorative treatment of form
at the expense of feeling attains full
expression in this work. His love for
ornamental detail is evident in the wealth
of jewelry and the richly-bordered skirt
worn by the dancer. Her mannered
gestures, and angular pose reflect the
sculptor's interest in the art and dance
forms of India; the treatment of the hair,
eyes and heavy draperies cascading from
her shoulders suggest archaic Greek
sources.
J.F.H.
L.A.K.

(see cover)
44. *Flight of Night,* 1916
gilded bronze, marble base
32 x 31 x 8
Collection Minnesota Museum of Art
Gift of Mrs. Arthur H. Savage
58.02.03
Murtha 81

Often considered one of Manship's most
elegant works, and an early expression of
his mature style, *Flight of Night* evokes
classical Greek and East Indian sources.
The allegorical figure of night floats in
space over the universe, suggesting
ubiquity, and her upraised arms round her
head echo the globe over which she hovers.
Her clearly delineated form suggests the
crescent shape of the moon; the crescent
moon was the ancient attribute of the
virgin. *Flight* looks back over her shoulder,
while her body moves forward with speed
to make way for the oncoming day; her
form is weighted toward the left,
heightening the sense of movement.
G.K.

The influence of India is discernible in Manship's work as early as
1913, in *Vase* with an oriental dancer (41). This motif was more fully
developed in *Salome* (43) 1915. With its ornament-encrusted surfaces,
Salome is among Manship's most overtly — one is tempted to say, overly
— decorative works. The sumptuous jewelry, costume and hairstyle
certainly evoke exotic lands and are, in Murtha's words, "entirely suitable
to the barbaric opulence of this theme."[23] However, the detail seems much
less *of* the form than overwhelmingly *on* it; viewing this work, one is
acutely aware of minutiae, at the expense of the whole. In this case,
Manship has not succeeded in achieving what the Indian sculptor so
brilliantly mastered: namely, to make detail subservient to mass.

Among Manship's works, *Dancer and Gazelles* (40) 1916, was perhaps
the one most frequently associated with the art of India. The connection is
far from obvious, but is most often evoked by the dancer's gesture; A.E.
Gallatin, for one, was reminded of "the significance that the Indian artist
attaches to gesture, as well as the symbolism of the hands."[25] While the
gesture made by Manship's *Dancer* defies specific interpretation, it
undeniably suggests the complex code of hand gestures — the *mudrās* —
that are so central to the dance, drama, fine arts and religion of India.[26]
These elements are most expressively combined in some of the most
famous of all Indian sculptures, showing the god Śiva as *Natarāja* — Lord
of the Dance.[27] Such figures move with an ease and grace that find few
parallels elsewhere; Manship's best archaistic works are among their closest
modern equivalents.

Manship's success with *Dancer* lies precisely in his ability to evoke,
rather than imitate. One feels that many forms and styles from the artistic
past contribute to its appearance, yet they do not explain its appeal. In
praise of this sculpture and its artist, a critic once wrote: "where joy and
life abound, conventions and traditions do little for the artist except to
free his creative force."[28] In *Dancer and Gazelles,* we see Manship as a
sensitive and receptive observer of art and an artist of independent vision.

The major stylistic elements of Manship's archaism were all manifest
in his work by the mid-teens. Once he had embraced the decorative and
linear aesthetic of pre-classical Greek art, it was but a short step to the
acceptance of other styles, which had been overlooked in the nineteenth-

45. *Diana,* 1921
bronze, marble base
36⅞ x 26¾ x 11⅝
66.14.103a
Murtha 138

46. *Actaeon,* 1923
bronze, marble base
30½ x 32 x 11¾
66.14.103b
Murtha 155

According to myth, Diana the chaste Roman goddess of the hunt transforms Actaeon, the hunter, into a stag because he inadvertently sees her bathing. Actaeon is shot by Diana and, as he gradually turns into a stag, is attacked by his own two hounds.

The arabesque curves of *Diana's* body are repeated in her flowing drapery. She is depicted at the moment she releases the arrow which has flown beyond view. As it leaves her bow, she glances back at her target over her left shoulder. Her body, suspended in a leap above ground, breaks into headlong flight; the dog beneath her echoes *Diana's* pose with head turned back and legs extended in a full run. Both figures are supported by stylized plant forms with curling leaves.

Contrasting with the linear quality of *Diana,* the sharp diagonal form of *Actaeon* is portrayed the moment after the arrow has struck his flesh. His body stiffens as he lunges forward, frozen in agony, his hand covering the wound to his side. His partially opened mouth further expresses his anguish. The dogs represented closely

resemble the Etruscan *She-Wolf*, that
nourished Romulus and Remus, with its
archaic traces in the tight curls and
stylized mane.

 Manship intended these works to be
shown as a pair. He had worked with the
themes as early as 1911. They reflect
Manship's mature style and are typical of
his manner of giving traditional elements a
modern appearance. The stylization of the
forms, the balance between linear
definition and silhouette, reflect his
affinity for archaic Greek vase painting,
(the subject of Actaeon has been depicted
by the Pan Painter, late 5th c. B.C.). The
emphasis on streamlined movement,
smooth surfaces and mannerist poses, place
the work within the prevailing Art Deco
style.
G.K.

47. *Frieze Detail From the Treasury of the Siphnians, Delphi,* 1912
pencil on paper
8½ x 6¼
66.14.152a

This is one of two drawings in MMA's collection of the Siphnian Treasury (66.14.152b), that Manship completed while a student at the American Academy in Rome. Drawn with meticulous care from a fragment of a carved stone frieze from an archaic Treasury at Delphi, Manship gives special attention to the architectural detail. He faithfully and with precision recreates the bead and reel design at the base and top, and in the center lotus, palmette and snail shell designs. G.K.

Frederick William MacMonnies
(1863-1937)
48. *Diana,* 1890
bronze
30½ high
Collection The Minneapolis Institute of Arts
Gift of Mr. and Mrs. Arnold Hobbs
64.62

The naturalistic style in this work is typical of the generation moving away from neoclassicism in the late nineteenth and early twentieth centuries and, in this sense, MacMonnies followed the lead of his teacher, Augustus Saint-Gaudens, who also sculpted *Diana* in a bold, realistic style.

Born in Brooklyn, MacMonnies studied in Paris at the École des Beaux-Arts. It was his *Diana* that received honorable mention at the Salon of 1889 and brought him

century bias toward naturalism. These included the arts of India and China, Egypt and Assyria, and of Romanesque Europe.

Manship was by no means the only artist to respond to such sources, nor were these alternatives to traditional forms and subject matter sought exclusively by sculptors. In the world of the dance, one need only consider the quasi-Indian productions of Ruth St. Denis, the bacchic movements of Isadora Duncan (which inspired Bourdelle's archaistic reliefs for the Théâtre des Champs-Elysées), and the mythological ballets of the Ballets

acclaim internationally.* In this work he presents a classical subject, but there are no neoclassical references. Her form is supple, graceful with slender proportions. Her softly modeled face and hair are realistic and individualized, whereas Manship's *Diana* (45), is more idealized. The only attributes that associate MacMonnies' *Diana* with antiquity are the bow and crescent in her hair. She seems delicate when compared with Manship's athletic *Diana*.

*Wayne Craven, *Sculpture in America*, rev. ed., (Newark, Delaware: University of Delaware Press, 1984), 420-21.

G.K.

Russes, in which choreography, costumes and set design (especially those of Leon Bakst) united to create a vision of archaic Greece.[29] The Ballets Russes' most notorious effort was, of course, *L'Après-midi d'un Faun* of 1912. In a radical break from the classical ballet, Nijinsky's choreography emphasized slow, earthbound, angular movements. The dancers, with their limbs aligned essentially along a single plane, suggest nothing so much as a collection of archaic sculptures — or figures from a Greek vase — come to life (Fig. 10). Further parallels for archaism could be sought in film (such as D.W. Griffith's *Intolerance* of 1916) or fashion (the designs of Mariano Fortuny, for example), but it is sufficient to observe that archaism was an international stylistic phenomenon, discernible in many media, between 1900 and 1925.

What Manship did was to develop a lighthearted and charming archaistic sculptural style, which found immediate popularity here and came to dominate American academic sculpture by 1925. By that time, however, Manship himself had largely exhausted the style; it might be argued that his archaism culminates in the splendid heroic-size sculptures of *Diana* (45) and *Actaeon* (46), from the mid-twenties. At the same time, these figures express such concerns of his sculpture for the next two decades as the expression of movement and a new interest in mass and monumentality. Some elements of Manship's archaism would remain, of course, most notably an interest in mythological subject matter; but, then again, this was shared by academics and *avant-garde* alike. It was the obviously archaistic mannerisms — for they were becoming just that — that Manship largely abandoned. Thus, we may remember him as at once the creator of an American archaistic style and its greatest exponent.

Susan Rather
Smithsonian Fellow
Ph.D. candidate, University of Delaware

Notes

1

The accepted dates for Manship's study at the PAFA have been 1906-1907, probably based on the artist's recollection, since the inscription "Paul Manship - Phila. - 1906-7 by himself - age 21 years" appears in his hand on a *Self Portrait* (1) in the NMAA's collection. However, Manship's student card (PAFA archives) indicates that he was registered for the 1907-1908 term only. These dates are supported by correspondence, newspaper items and contemporary exhibition catalogues. The artist must have inscribed the *Self Portrait* later; this would explain the inaccuracy, as well as changes in the last digit of his age (from 23 to 21 or 22).

2

From a paper given at the Art Students League, New York City, 1915 (hereinafter cited as ASL papers); Paul H. Manship Papers, Archives of American Art, Smithsonian Institution (hereinafter cited as AAA).

3

Charles H. Caffin, *American Masters of Sculpture* (New York: Doubleday, Page, and Co., 1913), 9.

4

Comment by an unnamed artist related by Carl N. Werntz, President, The Chicago Academy of Fine Arts, 9 November 1912; American Academy in Rome Papers (hereinafter cited as AAR), AAA.

5

The American Academy (founded in 1894) was closely modeled on the Académie de France à Rome, a venerable institution dating to the seventeenth century.

6

George Breck (Academy director from 1904-1909) to Francis Davis Millet (Academy trustee, executive secretary, and chief administrator), 5 May 1906; AAR.

7

George Breck, from a brochure on the Academy published by the Mural Painters, 1910, p. 4. Life classes were held informally at the Academy but, during Manship's tenure (when the Academy was still housed in the insufficiently large Villa Mirafiore), many of the artists' studios were not even on the premises.

8

Millet to William Kendall, 15 September 1908; AAR.

9

Herbert Adams (President of the National Sculpture Society) to C. Grant La Farge (Secretary of the Academy), 8 December 1913; Files of the American Academy in Rome, New York.

10

New York Tribune, 20 December 1913, 9.

11

Kenyon Cox, "Art: A New Sculptor," *The Nation* 96 (13 February 1913): 162-63.

12

An antefix from Gela is illustrated in my article "The Past Made Modern: Archaism in American Sculpture," *Arts Magazine* 59 (November 1984): 111-19.

13

Catalogue of an exhibition of sculpture by Paul Manship (New York: Berlin Photographic Co., 1916), 7.

14

Manship to Isidore Konti, (early spring 1912), Konti papers, AAA.

15
ASL papers, Manship papers, AAA.

16
Ibid. There exist drawings by Manship of painted details remaining on the kore here illustrated (Acropolis 594).

17
Quoted in Edwin Murtha, *Paul Manship* (New York: Macmillan, 1957), 11-12.

18
ASL papers; Manship papers, AAA.

19
Cox, "New Sculptor," 162-63.

20
Bulkeley Cable, "Three Special Exhibitions of Notable Works of Art are on View at City Museum," *St. Louis Republic,* 11 April 1915, sec. 2, 5.

21
Charles Caffin, "Great Promise Shown in a Young Sculptor's Work," *New York American,* 17 February 1913, 8.

22
Roger Fry, "Oriental Art" (four book reviews), *Quarterly Review* 212 (January 1910): 225-39. Even Fry, however, found much Indian art, and sculpture, in particular, to be alien and inaccessible:

It is at once stranger and more familiar than the art of China and Japan. More familiar in that it treats the human figure with a certain structural completeness which...at least recalls the general European tradition. Stranger in...the religious symbolism of Brahmanism...we stand aghast before certain many-armed and many-headed figures in which the ideas of Śiva and Vishnu are externalized (234-35).

For a fascinating study of changing reactions to Indian art, see Partha Mitter, *Much Maligned Monsters: History of European Reactions to Indian Art* (Oxford: Clarendon Press, 1977).

23
Murtha, *Manship,* 157, cat. no. 73.

24
This aspect of the Indian achievement was underscored by one of Manship's contemporaries, the sculptor Maurice Sterne. In an interesting assessment of Indian sculpture (which suggests the attraction it probably held for Manship), Sterne wrote:

Hindu sculpture...is frequently over-rich in detail, but there is an appreciation of the importance of larger mass, a rhythmic flow of motion, that is sinuous and sensuous. A vulgar elegance, it should probably be classified as 'arty' rather than as great art, and yet, when you examine closely the details of their art or their architecture, you are astounded with the meticulous craftsmanship, with the patience and genius of their makers, who must have loved details more than any other people (Charlotte Leon Mayerson, ed., Shadow and Light: The Life, Friends and Opinions of Maurice Sterne {New York: Harcourt Brace Jovanovich, 1952, 1965}, 92).

25
A.E. Gallatin, *Paul Manship: A Critical Essay on his Sculpture and an Iconography* (New York: John Lane, 1917), 5-6.

26
The unity of Indian arts and the importance of gesture were underscored by Ananda Coomaraswamy in the introduction to *The Mirror of Gesture* (1916), his translation of an ancient Sanskrit treatise.

27
The image of Śiva Nataraja came virtually to embody Indian sculpture after the publication of Coomaraswamy's most popular work in 1918, a collection of essays entitled *The Dance of Śiva.*

28
George Humber, "Paul Manship," *New Republic* 6 (25 March 1916): 208.

29
Bakst's stage and costume designs offer a provocative visual parallel to Manship indeed, and reviews of their works could almost be interchanged. Compare, for example, Caffin's words on Bakst — "With equal facility he has drawn into himself the spirit of classic Greece, Egypt, and India, the Middle Ages and realized it abundantly in new living forms" — with Beatrice Proske on Manship — "Manship has the rare gift of historical imagination. He can project himself into another culture [she mentions archaic Greece and the East], extract its essence, and make it his own" (Caffin, "Leon Bakst's Wonderful Designs," *New York American,* (3 November 1913), 6; and Beatrice Proske, *Brookgreen Gardens Sculpture* [Brookgreen Gardens, S.C.: Printed by order of the Trustees, 1943], 308). In the context of international interest in a more primitive ancient world and in the East, Manship and Bakst absorbed, adapted and transformed similar sources to create distinctive and evocative works of art.

49. *Study for the Bronx Zoo Gates,* n.d.
crayon on paper
13¾ x 16⅜
66.14.47

This is one of several preliminary studies owned by MMA for the Paul J. Rainey Memorial Gateway at the Bronx Zoo. It shows the proposed gateway in a finished state set within its historic surroundings. Manship has drawn in the natural terrain as it was then — broad, intersecting avenues shaded by trees in full bloom. Distinctive touches which enliven the entranceway are the low walls flanking the gates, and the vintage cars in the inner drive. The artist has highlighted the bodies of the animals framed by the lavish grillwork, and the grillwork itself, with deft touches of golden brown and light blue color.

With the exception of the lunette groupings of deer and bears, several changes may be noted between this proposed version, and the contemporary gateway. In the drawing, Orpheus holds his lyre and is framed within the stylized fountain of vegetation which tops the central tree. In the bronze gateway, a majestic lion now sits atop the tree. In the study, animals populate the branches of the tree. In the realized gateway, birds, instead of animals, now perch in the branches, and the trunk is supported by a tortoise. Manship also broadened the gateway by adding two more trees to the outer edges of the entrance.
L.A.K.
S.L.

Fig. 11
Paul J. Rainey Memorial Gateway, 1934
bronze
36' x 42'
New York Zoological Park, Bronx Zoo,
New York
Murtha 344

The gateway was commissioned by Mrs. Grace Rainey Rogers as a memorial to her brother, Paul J. Rainey, a big-game hunter, explorer and motion-picture photographer. (The Bronx Zoo benefited from many of Rainey's big-game expeditions.)

Located on the northern border of the Bronx Zoo (on Pelham Parkway), the gateway marks the formal entrance to the grounds. The double gateway is surmounted by two lunettes, containing bear and deer groups; it is flanked by three stylized trees populated by birds and animals. The lion tops the tall central tree, in keeping with his reputation as king of beasts and guardian of the entry way. A total of twenty-two animals are included.

Manship drew the animals from life, faithfully reproducing some animal celebrities of the park, such as "Buster" the giant Galapagos tortoise, who supports the three stylized trees; "Jimmy" the Shoebill stork, and "Sultan" the African lion. A group of black bears occupies the left lunette as one enters the gate, while the right is filled with a family of deer. A leopard at the left and a baboon at the right sit atop the side terminals.

Each animal or bird has been modeled in the round and is an individual sculpture. The gates are flanked by two granite gatehouses designed by Manship in collaboration with architect Charles Platt. Initially the gate was to be a wrought-iron structure with the details of birds and animals executed in bronze relief. When the actual dimensions were determined, however, it was evident that the use of iron would necessitate scaling down details. To avoid the loss of detail and to make the gate primarily a sculptural work, Manship decided to have it cast in bronze from life-size models.

A working model, three-eighths scale, was the largest Manship could assemble in his studios in New York and Paris. To make the scale models and execute the details full-size took nearly five years and the help of fifteen assistants. About two more years were required to cast the gateway in bronze and assemble the parts. Cast in Belgium, a total of twenty-eight tons of bronze were used to complete the project. When the time came for delivery, the first ship contracted had a hold too small to accommodate the large crates. When the gates finally reached this country they were loaded onto special trucks. These proved too large to pass through the Holland Tunnel; the crates had to be transferred to a small ship and towed up the East River, placed back on the trucks and finally delivered to the Park.

J.F.H.
G.K.
S.L.

50. *Black-Necked Stork*, 1932
bronze, marble base
16¼ x 3¼ x 3¼
66.14.05
Murtha 304

51. *Crowned Crane*, 1932
gilded bronze, lapis lazuli base
13¼ x 8 x 2⅞
66.14.59
Murtha 308

52. *Concave-Casqued Hornbill*, 1932
gilded bronze, granite base
9¼ x 10 x 3¾
66.14.62
Murtha 306

Manship always gave his birds and
mammals sharply individual personalities.
In every expressive sculptural detail, one
senses the alertness of the crane, the
menacing quality of the hornbill, the
gentle mien of the stork. The *Crowned
Crane* stands delicately balanced on its
right foot, lifts its left foot hesitantly in a
position of readiness, as if ready to fly if
challenged. The finely-shaped head is
crowned by a bristling mass of feathers.
The *Concave-Casqued Hornbill* squats
stolidly, hugging the ground, and
protecting its territory. The "casque" refers
to the helmet-like projection on top of the
bill. MMA also owns a larger version of
this work (66.14.39). Manship emphasizes
both the reedy legs and slender inquisitive
bill of the *Black-Necked Stork,* as well as
precisely defining its feathers.
L.A.K.

53. *King Penguin,* 1932
bronze, granite base
1 1¾ x 4⅛ x 4¼
66.14.63
Murtha 314

The King Penguin, actually a member of a variety of smaller-sized penguins, has a black head with yellow and orange spots on either side. The choice of an overall green patina has helped the artist capture the smooth, streamlined shape of the animal. Only selected details of the penguin's body have been suggested, and the lines which form around the chest and head suggest a different color, in keeping with this emphasis on contour. The outlined areas on either side of the head detail patches of distinctive coloration. The delicate ruffle of feathers above the webbed feet, and the curly brush of the upturned tail are finely crafted details.

There is a subtle humor apparent in both the jauntily cocked head, and the military posture. The animal stands smartly at attention, flightless wings neatly folded at its sides, as if awaiting the orders of a superior in rank.
L.A.K.

54. *Group of Bears*, 1939
bronze
33½ x 27 x 19
66.14.109
Murtha 396

The bear and deer sculpture groups were used interchangeably by Manship in the Bronx Zoo Gateway, where they are shown side by side in the upper lunettes (Fig. 11) and in groupings of three for the Osborn Gateway, Central Park.

Manship's study drawing of a single bear captures the deliberate quality of the bear with its lumbering movement. In the large bronze grouping of three bears, the forms are simplified to sleek roundness with only the necessary delineation of detail to indicate their personalities. In spite of the few details over their flowing, curved surfaces, the animals are remarkably lifelike. The middle bear stands upright, looking about with his paws held inward in a peaceful gesture. He is flanked by two bears down on all fours, who seem even more earthbound in this position by their rounded formations. Manship endows the bears with a humorous, yet dignified quality and, in his animal sculpture, evokes his earlier master, Solon Borglum, from whom he learned the basic principles of anatomy.
G.K.

55. *Group of Deer*, 1941
bronze
33 x 26½ x 17½
66.14.108
Murtha 421

In contrast to the bear drawing, the deer
drawing is more stylized and the animals
more angular in shape. The sculpted group
of deer fill the upper right lunette of the
zoo gate. Manship has captured the
sensitive, fragile quality of the deer, and
endowed them with an inherent sense of
alertness, as if they could alight from their
positions speedily. There is more detail in
the faces, but the overall depiction of the
animals is spare with little carving, and
recalls Nadelman's stylized deer with their
abstract curved volumes.
G.K.

56. *Baboon*, 1932
bronze, granite base
16¾ x 8¾ x 9¼
66.14.41
Murtha 322

57. *Study of Baboons*, n.d.
pencil on paper
3 x 5⅝
66.14.161b

The bronze sculpture of the baboon,
serving as a terminal side figure for the
Bronx Zoo Gateway, was modeled from
life. The creature is remarkably like the
Egyptian baboons of the Old and Middle
Kingdom art in pose and in its rounded,
compact form — even to the delineation of
features and treatment of hair. The
Egyptian Baboon of Thoth was the patron
of scribes and the god of writing. As part
of his classical studies curriculum,
Manship had traveled in Egypt and may
have seen and been influenced by these
works.

  These two baboons were study
drawings for the Bronx Zoo gates. With a
few spare lines, in a fleeting, quick sketch,
Manship captures the entire feeling and
personality of the animals, especially the
figure on the left with its arms wrapped
around its drawn-up knees. Also in MMA's
collection is *Study of a Baboon*,
(66.14.189a).
J.F.H.

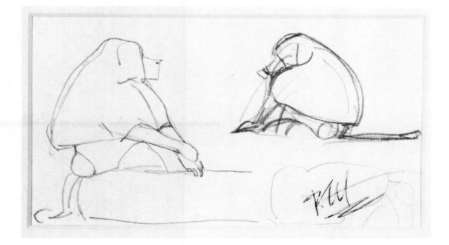

58. *Fawn and Deer,* n.d.
pencil on paper
4½ x 6⅝
66.14.129

59. *Bear,* n.d.
pencil on paper
4¾ x 6¾
66.14.132b

Fig. 12
William Church Osborn Memorial
Playground Gateway, 1952
bronze, marble posts
5'5" x 8' x 4"
Central Park, New York
Murtha 530

The Osborn Memorial Gateway features six
animal scenes from Aesop's Fables. The
gates were commissioned in honor of
William Church Osborn, President of The
Metropolitan Museum of Art.

    Manship created the gates in sections,
assembling them later. The *Group of Bear*
(54) and *Group of Deer* (55) placed on top of
the marble posts flanking the gateway (not
visible in this photograph) are identical to
those in the Bronx Zoo Gateway, where
they are shown individually. Also in
MMA's collection are two models for the
squirrels which top the gateway
(66.14.64a and b). The animals are
depicted in natural, active poses. They are
modeled in the round, silhouetted amidst
Art Nouveau foliage of flowers, vines and
tendrils and may be seen equally well from
either side of the gateway.
J.F.H.
L.A.K.

Fig. 13
Lehman Gates 1960-1961
bronze, granite base
18' x 26½' x 6'
Children's Zoo
Central Park, New York

Central Park's Children's Zoo, located near
65th Street and Fifth Avenue in New
York, was made possible by the generosity

of Governor and Mrs. Herbert H. Lehman.
The gateway created by Paul Manship was
commissioned in honor of the Lehman's
fiftieth wedding anniversary. Manship was
chosen because of his strong reputation as a
sculptor and for his achievement in
making two other New York gateways: the
Rainey Gateway in the Bronx Zoo, 1934
(Fig. 11) and the Osborn Gateway near
The Metropolitan Museum of Art, 1952
(Fig. 12).

Located at the entrance to the
Children's Zoo, the Lehman gates consist
of a long horizontal bronze sculptural
group supported by three large granite
pillars. The central pillar is the largest and
is inscribed with the following caption:
*Children's Zoo/For the Children of the City of
New York/by Governor and Mrs. Herbert H.
Lehman/1960.*

The horizontal sculptural group is of
children and animals playing music and
dancing. Running the length of the
gateway is an ornamental band of stylized
vegetation, populated by singing birds. A
boy sits on either end of the group playing
the pipes of Pan. In the center a boy and
two goats dance to the music of the pipes.
L.A.K.
S.L.

60. *Tortoise and Hare.* 1952
bronze, marble base
24 x 40 x 5⅞
66.14.36
Murtha 534

61. *Wolf and Lamb.* 1952
bronze, marble base
25¼ x 44½ x 6
66.14.37
Murtha 535

Manship and the Tradition of Garden Sculpture

62. *Venus Anadyomene*, 1924
bronze, marble base
11 x 6¼ x 4⅝
66.14.74
Murtha 171

Venus is the Roman goddess of love. The idea of two kinds of love, earthly and celestial, was formulated by Plato in the *Symposium*. Anadyomene is Greek for "borne of the sea."

This exquisite figure was executed as a study for a fountain at the Phillips Academy in Andover, Massachusetts. Her figure is not so robust as those seen in Greek and Roman sculpture. She is seen here bent over rather than in the traditional standing form, wringing water from her hair as she emerges from the sea. She kneels on her folded garments, presenting a compact sculptural form.

In the large marble version, Venus sits upon three concentric circular layers, supported by tall spiral pillars. The fountain was presented to Phillips Academy by former student Thomas Cochran of Saint Paul in 1929.
G.K.

At Brookgreen Gardens' dedication in 1931, Archer Milton Huntington stated:

> *Brookgreen Gardens is a quiet joining of hands between science and art…At first the garden was intended to contain the sculpture of Anna Hyatt Huntington. This has gradually found extension in an outline collection representative of the history of American sculpture, from the nineteenth century, which finds its natural setting out of doors…Its object is the presentation of the natural life of a given district as a museum, and as it is a garden, and gardens have from early times been rightly embellished by the art of the sculptor, that principle has found expression in American creative art.*

This tradition of art in gardens is as old as recorded history. The genius of Paul Manship retrieved the best ideas from archaic sculpture and vase paintings and fused them into a style that placed him in the forefront of American sculptors in the early twentieth century. Not only was his style derived from ancient motifs, but his sculpture is perhaps best seen outdoors as were those art works from which his inspiration was drawn.

In landscape architecture, the art of gardening and the science of architecture are combined to arrange growing trees, shrubs and other ornamental plants in connection with walks, drives and other features of the landscape so that together they form an artistic and pleasing view. Statuary obviously lends itself to this scheme.

Ancient outdoor sculpture was chiefly ornamental or religious in theme. There was, however, in ancient Greece and Italy, the widespread use of gardens as places for contemplation, relaxation and pleasure. Following the Greek example, Roman gardens contained a great deal of sculpture. Cicero wrote to his friend Atticus that he was awaiting the consignment of a sculpture for the garden of his villa at Tusculum; when it arrived he was so enchanted with its placement that he wrote, "…the whole place seems to exist for this statue alone."

Another feature found in Hellenistic gardens was the nymphaeum, a rocky grotto with running water, splashing and falling into decorated basins and shaded by trees or plant-covered pergolas. The use of the pergola had been borrowed from Egyptian gardens. Often containing statuary and always having decorative sculpture on columns, fountains and other architectural devices, the nymphaeum was a place for relaxation and

63. *Spring*, 1950
bronze
43 x 31½ x 18¾
66.14.107
Murtha 522

Spring is a cast of the gilded *Spring Fountain* (Murtha 508) completed in 1949 for Paul Manship's own garden in Lanesville, Massachusetts. According to C.G. Squire's essay on Paul Manship's outdoor sculpture, the 1949-1950 *Spring* is regarded widely as Manship's "foremost fountain figure."*

   A contemporaneous work by Manship, *Susanna* (Murtha 500), also a fountain sculpture, was commissioned by Houghton Metcalf of Middleburg, Virginia, in 1946 and completed in 1948. Both works express a new naturalism in the female figure — with its soft, rounded contours — which characterizes the artist's later work. This distinct change of style can be appreciated by comparing *Spring* and *Atalanta* (67) 1921. Both figures are running with draperies fluttering about them, but *Aatlanta* emphasizes the contour of the figure and its drapery while *Spring* is sculpted with a full three-dimensional naturalism.

   In *Spring*, the woman's drapery billows out spontaneously behind her back; it floats parallel to her outstretched arms helping to balance her body, the weight of which is borne by her left leg. Her right leg is positioned naturally, to help hold her balance bent slightly backward, as a wing is partially opened in flight.

   Manship's *Spring* is a young woman, in keeping with the symbolism of the season, as earlier expressed in Botticelli's

Primavera. A characteristic manifestation of spring, as personified in Manship's sculpture, is the presence of wind, suggested in the woman's fluid motion, backswept hair and flying draperies. The presence of a cherub blowing a long narrow horn further suggests the wind and is reminiscent of Cupid in Botticelli's painting.

*C.G. Squire, *Outdoor Sculpture by Paul Manship* (Wilton, Conn.: Kenneth Lynch and Sons, n.d.), 5, unpaginated brochure.

L.A.K.

S.L.

pleasure.

Fragments of ancient sculpture were found to be suitable ornaments for Italian gardens at the beginning of the fifteenth century. At this time, learned men and artists first created garden museums. The humanist, Poggio, set up antique statues in his garden, laid out c. 1483 at his villa in Terra Nuova. His statuary later passed into the Medicean collection, and with other acquisitions, formed the basis of this great grouping of art treasures. Cosimo and Lorenzo de' Medici both placed antique art works in their Florentine gardens. Lorenzo even established a drawing school in his garden where Michelangelo learned the art of sculpture from the study of these ancient statues.

Pope Julius II was an avid collector of statuary which he placed in the garden at the Penitentiary at San Pietro in Vinculi while he was still a cardinal. When he became pope, these pieces were transferred to the Vatican and placed in what is now the Belvedere Court, laying the foundation for what is considered the most important sculpture collection in the world. At that time (1523) the court was a garden. "Care was taken to consider the nature of each separate work; and in green surroundings, with running fountains and sweet odours, they gave a very different picture of beauty and poetry from that which they give today in their cold room indoors."

In sixteenth century England, Henry VIII enlarged Cardinal Wolsey's garden at Hampton Court. He built a "mount" on a foundation of bricks and earth, planted it with hawthorne and crowned it with a pavilion filled with heraldic beasts cut from stone and carved in wood. As well as the stone animals in Henry's garden, there were wooden cutout heraldic effigies of griffins, lions, fish, stars, shields and crowns mounted on poles. At the same time in Peru, the gardens of the Incas were adorned by representations of beasts, birds and plants made in pure gold and silver.

The greatest of the Jacobean gardens had elaborate waterworks designed by a French engineer named de Caux and an abundance of effigies and statues. During the Restoration in England, expensive waterworks were in vogue after the style of the French garden architect Le Nôtre, who designed the gardens at Versailles. Of importance in a French garden was not the garden but the fact that as a setting it enhanced the people who

64. *Study for Fountain Figure*
n.d.
pencil on paper
8¾ x 7¾
66.14.118e

In this drawing, a nude woman with flying
drapery is poised on a base encircled by
frog waterspouts. The figure and base are
set within a fountain basin. The woman
appears to be running rapidly, her drapery
billows upward, flying behind her. It coils
around her upper arms, and she grasps it
tightly with her hands, so as not to lose it.
The extended reverse diagonal of the right
leg effectively counterbalances the basic
verticality of the figure, giving it a feeling
of rapid forward motion. This type of
running figure, which emphasizes the
outlines of the forms, is also seen in
Manship's *Atalanta* (67) 1921.
L.A.K.
S.L.

walked and conversed in it. By the seventeenth century the English had
begun to shed ornamentation in the garden and to simplify. The Zen
Buddhist gardeners of Japan took this to an extreme, for their ultimate
garden was a space of raked gravel and a large rock correctly placed — the
art being in the placing of the stone. English gardens of the later
seventeenth century remained Italianate but with a purer, less baroque
taste. While masonry and waterworks were still important, they were used
formally rather than whimsically.

The English landscape gardeners of the seventeenth and eighteenth
centuries had much in common with the French landscape painters of the
period. They both created landscapes with natural materials but achieved a
more interesting and moving result than is usually produced by nature.
Especially characteristic of Chinese garden art during this period was its
intimate relation to painting. Among Chinese gardeners, the man who
sought and found a stone having the power in its shape to affect the spirit
like a work of art, was considered an honored artist. English landscape
gardening was based on the same principle.

The material of the landscape designer is alive and continually escapes
from his control; a garden whose trees are thirty years old does not look
like the same garden with trees one hundred years old. "...Nothing can
alter the fact that the changing light of the seasons alters what one is
looking at in a garden from day to day, and the skillful use of flowering
shrubs and trees recognizes that the material of which a garden is made is
alive and growing — an ever changing picture."[4]

The landscape designer can be said to be an artist in the sense that he
arranges the landscape to best advantage, taking into consideration the
effects of light, shade, growth and age of plants and placement of
decorative and utilitarian features. Paul Manship recognized that the most
important training a young sculptor could receive was to be able to design
an appropriate architectural setting, to envision how the sculpture will
appear in its setting, and to be technically proficient in all aspects of the
creation of sculpture.

The period from the end of the Civil War to the 1890s was one of
development and growth in American art. At the 1892 Columbian
Exposition in Chicago, Frederick MacMonnies' Columbian Fountain

65. *Study for a Fountain*, 1915
gilded bronze, bronze on marble base
12⅜ x 5¾ x 3⅞
66.14.93
Murtha 69

This small study for a fountain though
never realized in large scale, is similar in
conception to Manship's *Infant Hercules
Fountain* (Fig. 14) 1914, at the American
Academy in Rome. Similarities include the
depiction of a partially-draped figure on a
base set within an ornately-decorated
Renaissance fountain basin and two sets of
waterspouts — one on the base of the
sculpture and the other on the fountain
basin.

There are several contrasting features
between this study and the *Infant Hercules
Fountain*. The waterspouts in the fountain
study are all lion heads, unlike those
executed for the Rome fountain which
depict the Labors of Hercules. The
fountain for which this study seemed a
model was meant to be placed against a
wall, while the *Infant Hercules Fountain* is
freestanding.
L.A.K.
S.L.

66. *Female Figure with Flying Drapery,* n.d.
pencil on paper (cut-out)
5⅛ x 3⅞
66.14.170b

The nude female with flying drapery is a
subject which fascinated Manship
throughout his career. Achieving a sense of
balance and formal unity with the
elements of a figure in motion, swirling
draperies and a stationary base, tested the
limits of his skill with pencil and molten
metal. Some of his finest works, for
example *Atalanta* (67) 1921, and *Spring*
(63) 1950, show how masterful his
resolution of the formal problems
presented by this configuration could be.

In this drawing, Manship experiments
with the sphere as a base for a floating
female figure. The *Flight of Night* (44)
1916 (cover), represents the exquisite
resolution of the formal elements the artist
explores here. As in the finished sculpture,
the figure in the drawing hovers over the
spherical base not touching it with her
body; the draperies alone touch the sphere
and anchor the figure in space.
L.A.K.
S.L.

introduced outdoor sculpture as a form of entertainment. The formation of
country estates for the wealthy at this time created a demand for garden
sculpture and provided perfect settings to fire the sculptors' imaginations.
Recent art historians have stated that because the American public was
disenchanted with patriotism and the corresponding civic sculpture in the
aftermath of World War I, it was inevitable that Manship's style with its
elements of archaism, classicism and later streamlining, so different from
that of previous monumental works, would become popular. It was also
suggested that the trend toward the demand for sculpture to decorate
private gardens and estates began at this time. Here, Manship's genius
reached its apogee; the patronage of the wealthy assured his position.

Manship's style naturally lends itself to outdoor exhibition. His
enthrallment with Minoan art works and the archaic style sowed the seed
for his later preoccupation with works seen outdoors. A glance at Paul
Vitry's list of Manship's major works from 1911 to 1926 (which includes
some one hundred sculptures) shows that over one-third were originally
intended for outdoor exhibition. Most were of permanent materials that
could have been exhibited outside. His garden commissions by industrial
and business magnates from 1911 to 1917 and in the 1920s established
his clientele and prepared the ground for further commissions including
portrait busts, memorials and medals of the wealthy.

Among the commissions Manship received for garden sculpture
during the teens were several large projects offered to him on the advice of
such architects as Charles Platt and Welles Bosworth, who designed homes
and gardens for the affluent, and who knew and respected Manship's work.
Several of the larger commissions included the gardens of steel magnate
Charles M. Schwab, Loretto, Pennsylvania, for whom Manship created
several individual garden-size pieces including *Mother and Child,* 1917
(Murtha 90), *David as a Youth With Dog,* 1918 (Murtha 106), and *Hercules
Upholding The World,* 1918 (Murtha 107), as well as four large garden
vases made of lead with relief carvings, two terra-cotta flower boxes
(Murtha 91), two terminal figures, *Nymph* and *Silenus* (Murtha 93 and 94)
and a pair of limestone *Griffins,* 1917, later acquired for the collection at
Brookgreen. For the gardens of Harold McCormick, Lake Forest, Illinois,
Manship sculpted twelve large terminal figures and busts of Greek heroes

67. *Atalanta*, 1921
bronze, marble base
28¾ high
Collection Marion Koogler McNay Art
Institute, San Antonio, Texas
Gift of Alice N. Hanszen
Murtha 129

Atalanta, in Greek mythology, challenged
any man to run against her; the prize was
her hand in marriage. Since *Atalanta* was
very beautiful, many men tried the race,
and lost. One competitor, Hippomenes,
was given golden apples by Aphrodite,
which he craftily threw down along the
path as he and Atalanta raced. Pausing to
pick up the precious apples, Atalanta lost
the contest, and gained a husband.

Manship's *Atalanta*, shows the nude
young woman running, a piece of
fluttering drapery partially wrapped
around her left shoulder. The pose is
similar to that of the Giambologna bronze
statuette *Mercury*, another mythological
figure known for swiftness. The diagonal
position of the bodies, their sleek outlines,
and the sense of weightlessness in both
runners contribute to the feeling of swift
forward motion which animates both
works.

A small gilded bronze version of
Atalanta is in MMA's collection
(66.14.13).
L.A.K.
S.L.

68. *Grotesque Figure*, 1914
bronze, marble base
8¾ x 5¼ x 4½
66.14.28
Murtha 55

This cast is one of six identical waterspouts for Manship's *Infant Hercules Fountain* (Fig. 14), positioned directly under each of the six carved Hercules reliefs which encircle the base (69). The *Grotesque Figure* waterspouts are placed with their faces downward. In its vertical position, the figure is seated with his feet together, fingers interlaced, looking upward.

The surface of the *Grotesque Figure* is lightly embossed and engraved with leaves and flower petals, suggesting it is a type of garden deity. Its rounded, wide body and seated pose are reminiscent of Eastern sources.

The stylized beard with snail-shell curls suggest archaic Greek influences. The figure's large ears, rounded nose, and triangular beard are similar to *Centaur and Dryad* (42) 1913.
S.L.

and deities in 1914 (Murtha 61); and for Herbert Pratt, Glen Cove, New York, large versions of *Indian* (97) 1917, *Pronghorn Antelope* (98) 1917, *Duck Girl* 1911 (Fig. 6), and *Spirit of the Chase*, 1915. One of Manship's better-known patrons was John D. Rockefeller, Jr., for whom he made two terra-cotta flower boxes in 1916 (Murtha 87) as well as individual outdoor pieces in 1917 for Samuel Untermeyer, Yonkers, New York, and in 1916 for William Mather, Cleveland.

Other Manship outdoor commissions included sculpture for the New York World's Fairs in 1939 and 1964. The earlier Fair featured what was then the world's largest sundial, *Time and the Fates Sundial* (80), while the latter exhibited another Manship armillary sphere (Fig. 21). His penchant for time-keeping and astronomical devices was keen; he created several sundials, armillary and celestial spheres during his career.

In 1930, Archer and Anna Huntington purchased a rice plantation in South Carolina and conceived the idea of transforming the property into a sculpture garden of their own design which would incorporate the grounds of the plantation home. Ancient moss-festooned live oaks, boxwood, camellias, magnolias, crepe myrtles and podocarpus were residual plantings from the eighteenth and nineteenth centuries. The grounds of Brookgreen Plantation, planted by the colonists, followed the Italianate landscape tradition prevalent in eighteenth-century England. Anna Hyatt Huntington, a fine sculptor in her own right, and her husband, who was a scholar, poet and patron of the arts, intended to transform Brookgreen Plantation into Brookgreen Gardens where the finest pieces of American sculpture would be exhibited in outdoor settings. Their garden design, superimposed upon the original plantation, took the shape of a butterfly with outspread wings.

The intensively maintained gardens were contained within a pierced brick wall treated with a gray wash to complement the Spanish moss hanging in the trees. A variety of settings were created for appropriate sculpture to accent the landscape. Some settings surprise the visitor with a sudden view; others are more prominent where the garden unfolds a vista toward the accent sculpture. Cool white marble against vine-covered walls, splashing fountains, still reflecting pools, and vine-laden pergolas are a few of the classical elements of landscape design employed at Brookgreen

Fig. 14
Infant Hercules Fountain, 1914
bronze
figure approximately lifesize
Courtesy Trustees of the
American Academy in Rome, Italy
Murtha 54

Manship designed the *Infant Hercules Fountain* in 1914, and gave it to the American Academy in Rome the next year in appreciation of his three-years of study there. The fountain statue stands in the courtyard of the Academy complex on Janiculum Hill.

The figure of the young Hercules is strangling the serpent sent by Juno to destroy him in his cradle. According to Paul Manship's 1915 letter to the American Academy, this group "is intended to symbolize Youth's Triumph over Adversity." Encircling the base of the sculptural group are six bronze low reliefs of the Labors of Hercules, and below each relief is a grotesque figure waterspout. The figure and its base rest on a column, which is supported by a large saucer basin, ornamented with six lion-headed waterspouts.

The theme of the infant Hercules strangling the serpent is represented in ancient bronzes; an example is in the National Museum, Naples. Manship employs the spiral form as the basis of this composition, from the snake coiled around Hercules' massive club and layered about his upraised arm, to the contrapposto pose of the indolent young hero.

This fountain can be compared with Andrea del Verrocchio's *Putto with Dolphin Fountain* in the courtyard of the Palazzo

Vecchio in Florence. Similarities include the placement of the fountain in a courtyard, the elaborate ornate base, and the young male figure holding a struggling animal.
L.A.K.
S.L.

69. *Hercules Fights Triton*, 1914
bronze low relief panel
1⅞ x 4¾
66.14.228d
Murtha 56

MMA owns four bronze low relief panels, (66.14.228a-d) which are casts from the six Hercules reliefs on the *Infant Hercules Fountain* (Fig. 14) at the American Academy in Rome. One illustrates Hercules fighting Triton, the sea monster, whose upper torso is that of a human, and lower torso that of a fish. This episode cannot be termed one of the classic Labors of Hercules. It was, however, commonly represented on Black-Figure vases of the late sixth century B.C.

An example of a Black-Figure vase painting of Hercules fighting Triton is in the collection of the Badisches Landesmuseum in Karlslruhe, West Germany. Manship's familiarity with Black-Figure techniques and his own early drawing of a Black-Figure vase in NMAA's collection are indications that he studied Greek vases with care.

In both the panel and the amphora, Hercules is shown overcoming Triton, the gigantic sea monster, writhing in an agony of pain and defeat. A dolphin, one of the sea monster's traveling companions is shown swimming close to Triton's head in both vase and panel. Archaic Greek facial characteristics adapted by Manship include the almond-shaped eyes, and the stylized triangular beards.
S.L.

Gardens. Since its founding, Brookgreen has continued to grow and develop in the Huntington tradition. The sculpture collection currently includes 436 works of art by 197 artists; over two thousand taxa of native and exotic flora of horticultural interest to this region comprise the plant collection.

The Huntington idea of placing sculpture out-of-doors, borrowed from earlier civilizations, was to make the art works attractive to more people. Because individuals have varied interests, Archer Huntington felt that sculpture needed the background support of a garden and a garden needed the artistic accents of sculpture in order to appeal to a broad segment of the population. Gardens obviously differ from traditional museums in that lighting, weather and plantings change with the seasons; therefore, outdoor sculpture appears in constantly changing settings. As a sculptor, Paul Manship was cognizant of this phenomenon.

There are eighteen Manship art works in the collection of Brookgreen Gardens. The gilt bronze, *Diana* (45), and its companion piece, *Actaeon* (46), have fascinated artists, critics and laymen for nearly seventy years. The effectiveness of these art works is derived from the design of the silhouette against open spaces creating a lightness of form suggesting rapid movement but retaining monumental dignity. The first sketch of these pieces was done in 1915, just three years after Manship's successful New York exhibition which launched his career. Walker Hancock wrote:

Manship was the first to treat bronze as a hard material enhanced by the

Fig. 15
Attic Black-Figure Amphora
Hercules Fights Triton
Chiusi Painter, sixth century B.C.
Badisches Landesmuseum,
Karlsruhe, West Germany
61.24

70. *Labors of Hercules,* n.d.
pen and ink on paper
7 x 12¼
National Museum of American Art,
Smithsonian Institution
Gift of the Estate of Paul Manship
1966.47.242

In this drawing, Manship was sketching
ideas for Labors of Hercules themes, some
of which were realized in sculpture.

The drawings on the left depict
Hercules in fighting positions. The top
drawing shows Hercules in Greek battle
dress, the bottom drawing shows him
wearing the hide of the Nemean lion.

The top center drawing depicts
Hercules slaying the man-eating
Stymphalian swans with a sling-shot.
According to myth (the sixth labor of
Hercules), these swans, who inhabit Lake
Stymphalus, had claws and beaks made of
brass; their feathers were poisoned arrows.
Hercules frightened these birds into the air
with a rattle and killed them.

The mid-center drawing is of the
Chimera, a fearful monster with the head
of a lion, the body of a goat and the tail of
a serpent. The Chimera is usually
associated with Bellerophon who killed the
creature while astride the winged horse
Pegasus. The central bottom drawing
depicts Hercules battling with the Centaur
Nessus, who attempted to make love to
Deianeira, the wife of Hercules.

The top right drawing is of Hercules
struggling with Antaeus, a giant and
wrestler of Libya. He was invincible while
he touched the earth, which was his
mother, Gaea; Hercules strangled him
while holding him aloft.

The drawing on the bottom right
depicts Hercules slaying the giant
Alcyoneus; a herdsman who stole the cattle
of Helios.

The drawings appear to have been
rapidly done but, with just a few lines,
Manship expressed the complexities of
mythological themes.
J.F.H.

beauty of chased surfaces — his bronzes suggested in their flow of line the running of molten metal...Diana is the supreme example of this fluidity of line and reveals his debt to the Greek vase painters.[5]

At Brookgreen Gardens, *Diana* and *Actaeon* are silhouetted against the western sky overlooking the somber swamps and great bald cypress trees of the Waccamaw River flood plain. They were enlarged in 1924 from the 1915 sketches although Manship made several experimental studies before arriving at the final models. *Diana,* in heroic size (7'3") was finished in Rome; *Actaeon,* in progress at the same time, was completed in Paris.[6]

On the front wall of the sculpture garden at Brookgreen are the two *Griffins,* referred to earlier, looking across a circular pool. In mythology, the griffin was associated with gold and hidden treasure. Brilliant blooms of yellow jessamine on the wall in the spring imitate the golden treasure guarded by the mythological griffin. Manship's *Griffins* provide a second allegory in that they guard the gate to the sculpture garden and its hidden treasures that lie within for the enjoyment of the visitor. There is also an echo of the use of heraldic devices as decoration in the fifteenth-century Tudor garden.

Manship's *Flight of Europa* (15), is exhibited in the loggia, an open-air gallery around a rectangular pool. This gilt bronze was modeled in 1925 and depicts a portion of the story of the kidnapping and seduction of the Phoenician princess, Europa, by Zeus. Manship's *Flight of Europa* was inspired by Minoan works of art and derived from painted vases. Stanley Casson wrote of it:

the inspiration has not tyrannized over the artist for, from these Minoan sources, he has made an original work of great rhythm. The triangular shape of the whole composition brings with it great subtleties of balance in weight and in line.[7]

Gilded bronze castings of ten bird figures from the Paul J. Rainey Memorial Gateway at the New York Zoological Park decorate three areas of the sculpture garden. On pedestals surmounting brick columns on either side of the entrance gate are the *Owl* and *King Penguin* (53), *Goliath Heron, Crowned Crane* (51), *Flamingo* and *Adjutant Stork* mounted on pedestals at the entrance to the porch of the Small Sculpture Gallery. *Black-Necked Stork* (50), *Concave-Casqued Hornbill* (52), *Pelican* and *Shoebill Stork* adorn columns atop twin flights of stairs at the back wall of the garden. These

sketch for garden figure　　Paul Manship

71. *Sketch for Garden Figure,*
Satyr Playing Pipes, n.d.
ink wash and pencil on paper
7¾ x 6¼
66.14.197
Murtha, illustrated following pl. 70

This sketch for a fountain shows a Satyr
slightly off-center, yet delicately balanced.
He moves to the right playing his pipes,
unaware that he is about to step off the
base, yet his tail rests firmly on the left
side of the base, serving to anchor his
position. Manship's debt to red figure
Greek vase painting is seen in the line
detail of the musclature. The drawing is
freely executed, the dancing movement of
the satyr caught by the rounded arch
which frames the scene.
G.K.

staircases, beneath branches of flowering dogwood trees, lead to the former
rice fields between the upland plantation grounds and the freshwater tidal
creeks. The appropriate combination of the sculpture subjects and the
setting creates a most pleasing vista from the steps to the distant
landscape. The birds were modeled in 1932, part of a five-year commission
from 1929 to 1934 to design all of the animal figures for the Rainey
Gateway.

Cycle of Life Armillary Sphere (89), a gilded bronze sundial in the shape
of an armillary sphere, was originally designed in small size in 1920 and
cast in an edition of twelve examples. It was enlarged to just over five feet
in height in 1924 and three additional examples were cast including the
one in the collection of Brookgreen Gardens. The sundial and all of its
components symbolize the cycle of life encompassed by the cycle of
eternity. Here, "the sculptor's love of fine ornament expended itself on
such [an] individual conception...sparkling with gem-like reliefs..."[8] *Cycle
of Life* is exhibited in the formal Palmetto Garden which features a
rectangular pool, clipped holly hedges, and double rows of palmetto trees
lining rectilinear walks.

Another Manship time-keeping device is *Time and the Fates Sundial*
exhibited atop a small grass covered mound (reminiscent of the mount of
the Tudor garden). Commissioned for the 1939-1940 New York World's
Fair, this sundial is best described in the sculptor's own words:

The Perisphere & Trylon at the World's Fair suggest to me symbols of
measurement of Time & Space, so my sun-dial — "Time, the Fates and the Thread
of Life" — relates to the background of the central motif of the Fair — the
Perisphere & Trylon. Sun-Dial. The gnomon casts its shadow on the platform dial
surrounding it and registers sun-time. The gnomon is upheld by the Tree of Life,
which grows out of a rocky insular base. The Three Fates — Clotho, the Future,
holds the distaff and is the motif of the forward curve; Lachesis, the Present, is
vertical and looking ahead, and is measuring the thread as it passes through her
hands; Atropos, the Past, the curved line which returns within itself, symbolises the
end of things as she cuts the thread. Over her head the branches of the Tree of Life
have lost their foliage, and the Raven — the Bird of Doom — sits watching her.[9]

The gnomon casts its shadow on steel Roman numerals set in beds of
seasonal annuals and roses along the northern half of the walkway

encircling the sculpture.

Another art work from the 1939-1940 New York World's Fair is *Evening* (84), one of four elements of the fountain group, *The Moods of Time.* The other three figures were *Morning* (82,83), *Day* (85), and *Night* (86,87). Manship wrote that *Evening* symbolized inertia — "that time of inactivity before the movement of night begins, and the figure is falling asleep, with the shadows of evening over it." The observation of an art critic in 1935, although predating the study model of *Evening,* amply captures the feeling of the work: *Delicacy rather than brute strength appears to be the keynote of Manship's thought.*[10]

Paul Manship's work is well suited to placement in a garden. He said:
Sculpture is but a part of the greater scheme of art — dissociated from Nature, it still must find its rhythms in the organization of natural forms. Architecture and its abstract forms also belong to this large scheme to which the sculptor should devote his studies. But more important than formalities and geometrical considerations is the feeling for human qualities and harmony and movement of life.[11]

He lectured on various sculpture topics including Renaissance garden sculpture and contemporary garden sculpture. Manship urged the use of art works to decorate public parks as "permanent records of our times."[12]

Gurdon L. Tarbox, Jr., Director
Robin R. Salmon, Archivist
Brookgreen Gardens

Notes

1
Brookgreen Gardens History, Murrells Inlet,
S.C.: Brookgreen Gardens, 1954, 6.
2
Marie Luise Gothein, *A History of Garden
Art,* ed. Walter P. Wright and trans. Mrs.
Archer-Hind, I (Reprint. New York:
Hacker Art Books, 1966), 86.
3
Gothein, *History Garden Art,* 224.
4
Gothein, *History Garden Art,* 10.
5
Walker Hancock, *Fenway Court* (Isabella
Stewart Gardner Museum), vol. 1, no. 1
(October 1966), 3.
6
Beatrice Gilman Proske, *Brookgreen
Gardens Sculpture* (Brookgreen, S.C.:
Brookgreen Gardens, 1968), 290.
7
Proske, *Brookgreen Gardens,* 291. (Stanley
Casson, *Twentieth Century Sculptors,*
London: Oxford University Press,
1930,53).
8
Proske, *Brookgreen Gardens,* 287.
9
Sotheby Parke Bernet, New York, *American
Impressionist and Twentieth Century Paintings.
Drawings, Watercolors and Sculpture,*
exhibition catalogue, sale 4486M (4
December 1980), item 92. (The Paul
Manship Papers, NY 59-15:362, *The
Archives of American Art.*
10
H. Granville Fell, "American Sculpture in
London," *Connoisseur* 76 (August 1935),
101-02.

11
Hancock, *Fenway Court,* 7, 13.
12
"Leave the Sculptures," vol. 14, no. 20
(1 September 1940), 20.

72. *Study for Male Figure,*
Prometheus Fountain,
Rockefeller Center, 1934
bronze
9 x 14½ x 4
National Museum of American Art,
Smithsonian Institution
Museum Purchase
1971.13
cf. Murtha 339

73. *Study for Female Figure,*
Prometheus Fountain,
Rockefeller Center, 1934
bronze
9 x 13 x 3¾
National Museum of American Art,
Smithsonian Institution
Museum Purchase
1971.14
cf. Murtha 340

These two studies for the figures of
mankind flank the Prometheus sculpture
in the Rockefeller Center fountain. These
mankind figures represent the first human
beings created by Prometheus.

The studies are almost identical to the
finished sculptures. In the fountain
installation the male figure is placed on
the left and the female figure on the right.
Both figures are represented semi-nude;
each holds out one hand, waiting to receive
fire from Prometheus. The figures rest
against vegetation which may symbolize
their birth; Manship used similar
ornamentation in *Diana* and *Actaeon* (45)
and (46).
S.L.

Fig. 16
Prometheus Fountain, 1934
gilded bronze, granite base
18 feet high
New York, Rockefeller Center
Murtha 338

Paul Manship received the *Prometheus Fountain* commission on 30 January 1933, and the work was dedicated on 9 January 1934. The fountain is located against the western wall of the sunken plaza in front of the RCA building in Rockefeller Center.

Prometheus is known in Greek mythology as a Titan, who created man from earth and water. The most famous of his deeds was the bringing of fire from heaven to mankind. He was punished for the theft of fire by the father of the gods. Zeus had him chained to a rock where an eagle devoured his liver day after day. Eventually, Hercules freed Prometheus from his torture.

The recently regilded *Prometheus* depicts the bringing of fire to mankind. Below him is a ring on which the signs of the zodiac appear in low relief. He is supported by a rock-like structure representing a mountain. His body is stylized and smooth-surfaced, but his hair is a mass of upswept flames.

Flanking Prometheus are two recently reinstalled figures of a man and a woman representing mankind. In 1935, the *Boy* (72) and *Girl* (73), were placed in the Roof Garden of the Palazzo Italia, which faces Saint Patrick's Cathedral. In 1984, these figures were reinstalled near Prometheus. They are at ground level rather than elevated close to the Prometheus figure, as was Manship's original intent. The *Boy* and *Girl* are partially draped and rest against decorative curving vegetation.
S.L.

74. *Prometheus,* 1933
gilded bronze, marble base
7¾ x 6⅝ x 3⅛
66.14.96
Murtha 337

This study for the Rockefeller Center
Prometheus is the only gilded bronze study
known for the heroic work. Although the
study is not a clearly chiseled bronze, it
shows Prometheus flying in a horizontal
position and forecasts the streamlining in
the finished work. In the study the zodiac
ring is not present, and a fiery torch,
instead of the Titan's bare hand brings the
fire directly.
L.A.K.
S.L.

75. *Prometheus Studies,* c. 1950
pencil on paper
11 x 8½
66.14.196c

These five sketches are studies for the
bronze *Prometheus Trilogy* (77, 78, 79). The
most detailed sketch on this sheet is of the
"Fire Giver." As in the 1950 bronze
version (77), this sketch shows Prometheus
bearing a fiery torch while running on a
cloud-topped mountain. In the drawing,
Prometheus wears drapery, which flies
horizontally as it does in the *Prometheus
Fountain.*
  Prometheus Bound (78) is represented
twice in this drawing. The version titled
Bound is lower center left, and is
compositionally similar to the finished
bronze. In this sketch, Prometheus half
kneels with his back against the rock, the
eagle perched on his shoulder.

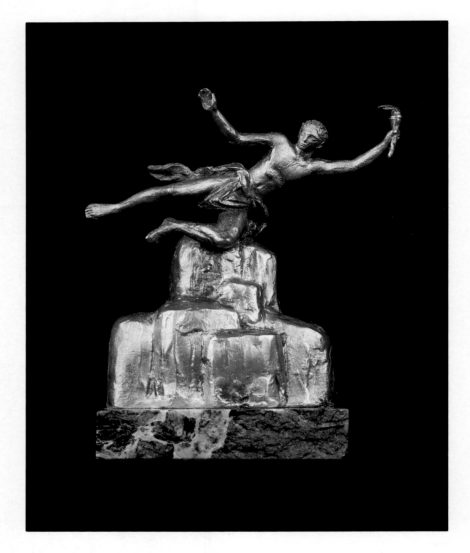

The sketch for *Prometheus Freed by Hercules* (79) in the lower left corner of the page, differs from the finished sculpture. Hercules wears the Nemean Lion's skin and does not carry a club as he does in the bronze.

These sketches were drawn on the back of stationery from the Office of the President of the American Academy of Arts and Letters. Manship was the President of this organization from 1948 through 1952, which suggests the dating for these sketches.
L.A.K.
S.L.

76. *Prometheus Bringing Fire*, n.d.
ink, pencil, crayon on paper
9½ x 12¼
66.14.130a

The legend of Prometheus bringing fire to mankind is written above this drawing:
Prometheus brought the fire that hath proved to Mortals a Means to Mighty Ends.

A similar inscription is on the wall behind the *Prometheus Fountain* in Rockefeller Center.

Mankind is symbolized by the miniature figures below Prometheus'. Two of the humans crouch in fear, while the other four hold out their hands anxious to receive the gift of fire. Unlike the *Prometheus Studies* drawing (75), this sketch is executed in an angular and stylized technique.
S.L.

77. *Prometheus Bringing Fire,* 1950
gilded bronze, marble base
9¼ x 4¾ x 4⅛
66.14.88c
Murtha 516

78. *Prometheus Bound,* 1950
gilded bronze, marble base
9⅝ x 4⅛ x 4⅛
66.14.88a
Murtha 517

In 1950, seventeen years after the *Prometheus Fountain* commission, Paul Manship made these three studies illustrating the Prometheus legend. The group is called the *Prometheus Trilogy.*

In the sketch *Prometheus Bringing Fire,* the Titan is depicted running on a mountain in the clouds. He carries a burning torch instead of bringing fire in his bare hand.

In the sketch depicting *Prometheus Bound,* he is shown with his wrists and ankles chained to a rock. Prometheus' tortured pose, with legs bent backward against the rock and head gripped by the eagle's claw graphically depict the pain he is experiencing.

In *Prometheus Freed by Hercules,* Hercules is shown helping Prometheus to his feet, having just freed the Titan of his chains. Hercules can be recognized by the knotted club which he carries over his shoulder, and is similar to MMA's bronze sketch of *Hercules,* 1945 (66.14.58).
S.L.

79. *Prometheus Freed by Hercules,* 1950
gilded bronze, marble base
8⅛ x 4⅛ x 4⅛
66.14.88b
Murtha 518

Manship's Once and Future Reputation

This is a bronze sketch of the work commissioned for the 1939-1940 New York World's Fair. It is the larger version of two in MMA's collection (66.14.104). The white molded plaster version (Murtha 390) exhibited at the Fair near the Trylon and Perisphere had a prominent central location. Advertised as the "world's largest sundial," the gnomon was eighty feet in length.

The three female figures represent the Three Fates of classical mythology: Clotho, the Spinner who represents the Future, holds the distaff and spins the thread of life; Lachesis, the Disposer of Lots or the Measurer who represents the Present, measures the thread as it passes through her hands, assigning to each person his or her destiny; Atropos, the Cutter, who represents the Past, symbolizes the end of things as she cuts the thread of life at death. The gnomon rests on the Tree of Life and casts its shadow on the platform dial surrounding it to register the sun-time. The Tree of Life bears leaves over the Future and Present scenes but is bare over the Past. The raven, symbol of Death, watches the cutting of the thread of life.

Manship's treatment of faces and hair as well as the slight stiffness of the figures recalls archaic Greek art.
J.F.H.

First the happy news: Paul Manship still has reputation enough for us to celebrate the centennial of his birth. Now the sad news: his sculptures, which made him the best-known American sculptor in the 1920s and 1930s, look only a little better than they did in the 1950s and 1960s, when he virtually disappeared from view.

Why was his work once so esteemed? Why did it then drop from favor? Why isn't it better thought of now? These are questions each essay in this catalogue tries to answer. But they are not merely academic questions. They are questions many viewers of Manship's centennial exhibition will ask themselves, because his lost celebrity raises doubts about not only the durability of art but our mortality and how we deal with it.

I

From the godly perspective of hindsight Manship's career makes perfect sense; we can understand why his relation to his audience was as it was. He came to prominence in the early decades of the century by doing in sculpture what many other artists — painters, photographers, writers, dancers — were doing in their media: offering a tasteful vision of classic or exotic life. His purpose wasn't that of the period's progressive artists and muckraking writers: to reform American life. It was to create beauty; to provoke nostalgia, romance and libidinous thoughts; to astonish with technical dexterity; to entertain.

What Manship did in sculpture for the most cultured audience, his good friend Maxfield Parrish was doing in illustrations for the mass market, Ruth St. Denis was doing in pseudo-Egyptian dances for vaudeville crowds, the Photosecession photographers were doing in pictures aping Ancient Greece and the Old Masters. It was the age of eclecticism. The Robber Barons were bringing home the plunder of the great civilizations and putting the pieces in museums, under glass and guards.

There have been few explanations of why ersatz exotic art was so popular in the decades around 1900. The best explanation so far sees this art as a response to the immense amount of social change going on: the

Fig. 17
Paul Manship, *Time and the Fates Sundial*,
1939-1940 New York World's Fair, plaster
(destroyed)

81. *Sketch for the Time and The Fates,* n.d.
ink and pencil on paper
7⅞ x 9½
66.14.128b

The treatment of the leaves in this drawing
has changed in the bronze sketch. Instead
of the large, single leaves depicted in the
drawing, the bronze sketch shows a more
realistic treatment with small branches and
clusters of leaves.
J.F.H.

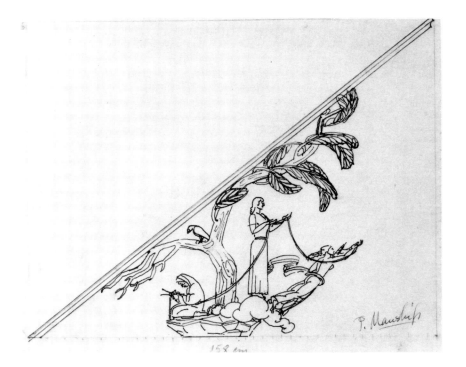

growth of industrialization and the city, the pauperization of the work
force and labor's consequent unrest, the flood of "new" (i.e., non-Anglo-
Saxon) immigrants, the waning of religious belief among the educated
classes. The literary historian James Vickery, trying to account for the
huge popularity of *The Golden Bough* (1890-1915), Sir James Frazer's
compendium of primitive myths, says that it "catered to the age's need to
escape from the spectacle of ignorant, deluded masses mired in economic
and moral squalor, the bourgeois vulgarized by the plutocratic exploitation
of others, and an industrial empire whose ugliness was in direct ratio to its
power."[1]

So, I would argue, with Manship's art. It didn't deal with society's
problems, as the Progressives tried to; it pretended the problems didn't
exist. It cast its glance backward toward a Golden Age.

Fig. 18
View of Central Mall, 1939-1940
New York World's Fair, *Time and the Fates
Sundial* and *The Moods of Time*

Fig. 19
Time and the Fates Sundial, view of Trylon
and Perisphere

THE MOODS OF TIME

The Moods of Time fountain group was executed in plaster in monumental size in 1938 and destroyed after the 1939-1940 New York World's Fair. Manship represented the four times of the day in allegorical form. The grouping was centrally located, close to the Trylon and Perisphere, in a rectangular pool near the *Time and the Fates Sundial* (Fig. 17, Murtha 390).

The "World of Tomorrow" was the theme of the fair, and the following description of Manship's *Moods of Time* appeared in *Art News,* 25 May 1940:

Considered by many his most important work of recent years, this fountain group is conspicuous for its freshness and vigor. The illusion of pace is cleverly sustained by the moving waters below and spray through which these figures actually seem to fly. It is appropriate that speed should figure in the World of Tomorrow.*

MMA's four sketches for the *Moods of Time* (82, 84, 85, 86) 1937, are unique and the earliest known bronze studies for the World's Fair fountain group. Other larger studies were completed in 1938 which closely resemble the final plaster versions. Murtha describes the two 1938 groups of studies as "scale models" and "working models." Examples of the "scale models" are the group in the collection of the NMAA.

**Art News,* vol. 38, no. 34 (25 May 1940), 14.
S.L.

That the Golden Age was phony goes without saying. The striking thing for us looking at Manship's art now is how little he himself seems to have cared whether or not his myth was true. The fierce conviction we see in primitive or classical works of sculpture — the sublime confidence that the world is just *this* way and no other — is generally absent from his work. His statues indicate who they are without somehow *being* the people. His *Salome* (43) 1915, is his *Lyric Muse* (9) 1912, is his *Dryad* (42) 1913, is his sleepy *Day and the Hours Sundial,* and *Flight of Night* (44), both 1916, is his *Dancer and Gazelles* (40) 1916, is his *Briseis* (99, 100) 1916 and 1950, *Atalanta* (67) 1921, and *Diana* (45) 1921, except that *Salome* is dressed in a rakish Art Nouveau costume with bare bejeweled breasts and a flapper waist, and she is doing a ragtime dance step called twenty-three skiddoo, quite as much as she is doing an East Indian dance. Like most of Manship's people, she is a performer.

With few exceptions, of which the John D. Rockefeller bust, 1918, is the most notable, Manship's statues don't have individualized faces. In this respect Manship was of course being faithful to classical and pre-classical art. But there is another reason for his abstracted faces; he wanted viewers' attention given to his bodies. His art celebrating the Golden Age was meant to be physical, erotic, and his vision of Eros was exactly that of the British Poet Laureate, Robert Bridges, whose "Eros" (1899) asks the god:

Why hast thou nothing in thy face? . . .
Surely thy body is thy mind,
For in thy face is nought to find,
Only thy soft, unchristened smile.

That soft smile plays about the lips of Manship's people, but though he made his fame depicting sensuality, he didn't really believe in it either. He was not a D.H. Lawrence nor — to choose an artist from his art, indeed his atelier — a Gaston Lachaise. He exploited sexuality and the Golden Age because they sold, not because their promise touched him deeply. In one of his most revealing comments he speaks of there being "a considerable feeling of humor" in "the antics of the heroes and gods of the ancient Greeks" and says that myths like Diana and Actaeon (a mortal who, having offended goddess Diana, is torn apart by his hounds) are "lots of fun" because they "combine animal forms with the human form."[2] Form

82. *Morning,* 1937
bronze, wood base
7⅛ x 5½ x 2⅛
66.14.81a
Murtha 369

I have tried to make these groups understandable to the average person, and, in Morning, which is awakening energy, use of the cock, the trumpeter and the throwing aside the veil of night is rather obvious." *

In both studies for *Morning,* the male figure is shown waking up. He yawns sleepily, and lifts the drapery, symbolizing the veil of night, over his head. An attendant assists him, and a rooster and trumpeter announce the arrival of day. In the 1938 version, the drapery is modified so that it billows out in an arch above the figure's head. The drowsy heaviness of the man's movements, as he stretches, and struggles to open his eyes, contrasts sharply with the crisp alertness of the three messengers of the dawn.
*The Paul Manship papers, NY 59
15:362, Archives of American Art.
L.A.K.
S.L.

counted for Manship; content mattered much less.

He believed in doing work that sold; in the teens and twenties what made his work sell was its archaizing sensuality. He must have realized this, but his claim was always that what made his art successful was its technique. Frederick Leach has suggested that Manship's journals are recipe books of sculptural techniques in which he jots down notes on how to achieve certain effects as well as the names and addresses of workmen he may want to hire again. The journals and Manship's few comments on his art show that his central value was craftmanship. He thought the best way for artists to be trained was through apprenticeship in a master's atelier, because young people "had not [the] thought to create works of art themselves" and "this education fitted them as expert craftsmen."[3] Never having been to college, he distrusted higher education and said, "Rather than theoretical book learning, the university should stress the craftsmanship of the artist."[4]

To praise craftsmanship was to praise himself — and not only because his name was in the word. Manship was a superb technician. But his emphasis on technique is troubling because he never speaks about the use

118

83. *Morning,* 1938
bronze, marble base
26¾ x 23 x 8¼
National Museum of American Art,
Smithsonian Institution
Gift of Paul Manship
1965.16.48
Murtha 381

to which technique is put. His fetish for craftsmanship is similar to that of
the economist Thorstein Veblen, whose *Instinct of Workmanship and the State
of the Industrial Arts* (1914), argues that people really want to do things
well but does not explain why therefore so much is done badly. Manship
and Veblen's celebration of craftsmanship was, I suggest, a convenient
refuge for skeptics so disillusioned they believe in doing things well,
whether or not the things deserve to be done.

2

When Manship returned to the U.S. in 1912 from his three years in
Rome, his work was welcomed by academics because it treated the Golden
Age and by fans of the *avant-garde* because it was somewhat abstract,
rather like Art Nouveau. Through his study of Oriental, (mainly Indian)
sculpture, he had learned how to use firm, patterned outlining, instead of
modeling, to define shapes. "An entire statue," he later wrote, "can be
considered as a decorative form upon which all the detail is drawn rather
than modeled."⁵

84. *Evening*, 1937
bronze, wood base
7⅞ x 5½ x 2⅛
66.14.81c
Murtha 368

Evening symbolizes inertia — that time of inactivity before the movement of night begins, and the figure is falling asleep with the shadows of evening over it. *

Differing from later versions, *Evening*, 1937, includes tiny sandmen, burdened with heavy sacks, kneeling on the female figure of evening, which suggests the heaviness of the approaching night. In the later versions of *Evening,* these small figures are replaced by flying owls, which give the grouping a less earth-bound quality.
*The Paul Manship papers, NY 59:15
362, Archives of American Art.
L.A.K.
S.L.

In the 1920s and 1930s Manship's tight forms and sharply defined outlines were perceived as belonging to the modish style of the day: streamlining. His popularity, already great, increased. In 1933 Royal Cortissoz, America's leading art critic, called him "the most successful sculptor in the country — the sculptor to whom all the important jobs naturally gravitate."[6]

As the cultural historian Jeffrey Meikle has argued, streamlining became widespread during the Depression because the practitioners of a new discipline, industrial design, argued that upbeat repacking was the way to revive American confidence and economic activity.[7] Things were restyled into streamline to make them look fresh, bold, clean and "scientific" — modern, impersonal, authoritative.

With the exception of his *Bronx Zoo Gates* (Fig. 11) 1934, Manship's notable public commissions of the period — the thirteen-foot-high statue *Abraham Lincoln — The Hoosier Youth* (88) in Fort Wayne, 1932; the monumental *Prometheus* in Rockefeller Center (Fig. 16) 1934; and several statues at the 1939-1940 New York World's Fair (82-87) — were in the streamline style and, to our eyes now, suffer from it.

Manship's Lincoln is a pretty boy with ultra-smooth pants. One of his

85. *Day,* 1937
bronze, wood base
9⅜ x 6⅝ x 2⅛
66.14.81b
Murtha 367

*On rushing Day, with the sun, typifies the date
of Helies [sic] with energy, radiation, speed.**

In Greek mythology, Helios is the sun
god who drove his chariot daily across the
sky; Manship portrays Helios running
while holding the sun in his outstretched
hands. The three curving wires present in
this version bend in the opposite direction
of the young Helios and represent either
chariot rails or sun rays.

The strongly diagonal running stance
of Helios suggests extreme speed. In the
1938 versions, this suggestion is reinforced
by the more pronounced, angular lines of
the sun god's drapery and hair. This
symbolic manner of indicating both speed
and fire is also evident in the Prometheus
figure in the drawing *Prometheus Bringing
Fire* (76), whose hair also resembles a mass
of flames.
*The Paul Manship papers, NY 59:15
362, Archives of American Art.
L.A.K.
S.L.

ankles is crossed over the other. His face has been retouched, the features
blurred as though dipped in acid. It is impossible to believe this soft
fellow could go through what the real Lincoln went through — and maybe
this means the statue works: by not showing the Lincoln who suffered it
reminds us of him. Still, a memorial statue that achieves its effect by
making us say "That's not the man" is an odd sort of triumph.

The gilded *Prometheus* provides a welcome burst of color, like a sun
rising over iron mountains, in the huge drabness of its location. It is, as
the architectural historian William Jordy suggests, a superb visual
magnet. But it is a silly statue (Jordy calls it "tawdry"),* surrounded by
silly drapery and a silly gold ring, the back part of which looks like the
handle of a fry pan. The statue's body is sleek and flabby, though its left
arm has a nice floating quality. The face is expressionless (as usual with
Manship), and the hair, in an exaggeration of classical style, is clumps of
curls and looks to our eyes like a 1960s bathing cap with plastic frills. The
theft of the gods' fire and the bringing of it to humankind is, as Manship
pictures it, about as agonizing and exciting as the delivery of a plate of
lettuce.

Manship's forty-eight-foot-high *Time and the Fates Sundial* (Fig. 17) at

86. *Night,* 1937
bronze, wood base
7⅞ x 5⅛ x 2⅛
66.14.81d
Murtha 370

On the other hand, Night, with the moon as its symbol, suggests the movement of the world of dreams and intangible things. The little figures accompanying the major nude figures of Night typify those things that reach out into space.*

In the 1937 depiction of *Night,* an allegorical figure of a partially-draped female lies on her back with her elbows bent and her hands cradling her head. The woman appears to be asleep; two streamlined flying male figures, positioned near, hover over the woman's body. Her upper body is flanked by stars and the crescent moon, which appear to shelter and support her in sleep.

Later versions of *Night,* as represented in the NMAA 1938 work, are characterized by a sense of weightlessness, movement and cleanly drawn outline. Instead of sleeping, the woman in these versions leans forward and stretches upward while her hair and drapery ends are swept to one side. The small flying male figures are placed above and below the woman's body which helps to balance the composition. There are obvious similarities to *Flight of Night* (44) 1916, in the sense of speed and movement.
*The Paul Manship papers, NY 59:15 362, Archives of American Art.
L.A.K.
S.L.

the World's Fair was built of plaster and destroyed at the Fair's end. No great loss: photographs suggest it was gawky and insipid. Manship's *Moods of Time* (82-87) sculptures from the Fair are allegorical streamlined gods — *Morning, Day, Evening, Night* — with smooth bodies and empty faces. Beneath each god is a pillow of clouds that resemble soft lumps of human flesh (there are many curled navels); these forms seem to have been inspired by the swatches of boneless bodies in Salvador Dali's paintings of the thirties.

After the 1930s Manship continued to work in variants of the streamlined style for the rest of his life, and his reputation plummeted. The entire streamline movement fell out of favor, as American artistic and popular taste in the 1940s and 1950s turned toward darker, freer, more emotional and individualistic styles. I am convinced — though this is not the sort of thing one can prove — that the main reason for this change of taste was World War II and the horrors committed by Nazi Germany.

It has been little acknowledged that the streamlined style in the U.S. owed a great deal to the totalitarian aesthetics of Hitler's Germany, Mussolini's Italy, and Stalin's Russia.⁹ Like the art promoted in these countries, America's streamlined art intended to be "public" —

87. *Night*, 1938
bronze, marble base
16½ x 24½ x 6½
National Museum of American Art,
Smithsonian Institution
Gift of Paul Manship
1965.16.47
Murtha 384

immediately comprehended by the masses — and heroic, orderly, affirmative and impersonal. The best instance of Manship's combining streamlining with European-style social realism is in his Anzio Monument (1953), which shows two GIs — idealized, empty-faced, shirtless young Aryans — walking arm in arm. Though American streamlining was hardly vicious in its ideological goals (it was used to sell toothpaste, autos and the New Deal), it was, like the European "mass man" art styles that influenced it, an aesthetics of control.

The war over, art used for such mass manipulation seemed crass and morally compromised. Streamlining itself looked too much like the work of the enemy we had defeated (Fascism) or the enemy pounding at our door (Communism). Post-war art in America became esoteric, one could argue, to *protect* it from the masses and from politicians who might use it as a means of misleading them. It became exactly what streamlining wasn't: anguished, raw, pessimistic, private.

3

Manship's reputation simply couldn't survive such an upheaval in taste. In the years between the early forties and the late fifites when high-culture

88. *Young Lincoln,* 1929
bronze
18 x 7 x 8
66.14.07
Murtha 252

This sketch is a study for the twelve-and-
one-half-foot sculpture *Abraham Lincoln:
The Hoosier Youth,* (Murtha 293),
commissioned by Lincoln Life Insurance
Company, Fort Wayne, Indiana. The
building architect, Benjamin W. Morris,
recommended Paul Manship for the
commission as he considered Manship "the
world's greatest living sculptor." The work
was modeled in Manship's Paris and New
York studios and cast in Brussels.

Lincoln lived in Indiana from age seven
to twenty-one. As there were no
photographic records from which to work,
Manship sought the assistance of Dr. Louis
Warren, an authority on the genealogy of
the Lincoln and Hanks families. To
familiarize himself with the subject
Manship toured the region where Lincoln
had lived, read widely, talked with Carl
Sandburg, noted Lincoln scholar, and other
Lincoln historians.

Lincoln National suggested Manship
depict Lincoln as representing the thought
of Emerson paraphrased:[1] *The World will see
the poet, the prophet, the thinker, even though
the path to his door led through the
wilderness.** The sculptor depicts Lincoln as
a young frontiersman leaning on an oak
stump. One hand is on the head of a dog
seated beside him, the other holds a
partially closed book. An ax rests against
his right leg. Manship found the dog he
used as a model for Lincoln's dog in
Kentucky and took the animal to Paris

with him. In early sketches Manship depicted Lincoln wearing moccasins and suspenders. Later the moccasins were changed to boots and the suspenders eliminated. Lincoln's homemade shirt and buckskin trousers emphasize his rural background.

The heroic-size bronze has allegorical reliefs representing the virtues most closely associated with Lincoln on each side of the pedestal: *Patriotism, Justice, Charity* and *Fortitude.*

Manship spent four years on the project; the resulting sculpture remains one of his most successful large works.
*Franklin B. Mead, *Heroic Statues in Bronze of Abraham Lincoln (The Hoosier Youth of Paul Manship),* The Lincoln National Life Foundation, (Fort Wayne, Indiana, 1932), 14.
J.F.H.

critics were excited by Existentialism, Kafka, Henry James, Jung, psychoanalysis, tragedy, the problem of evil, Neoconservative Christianity, candid photography, newsreels, Humphrey Bogart, *film noir,* Surrealism and Abstract Expressionism, his art looked sappy, pointless.

Are we today able to take a more balanced view of his work? Perhaps. Though we still honor the values and taste of the tragic modernists of a generation and more ago, we are ready to admit they don't give us the whole of life. Art can bring us simpler gifts than the modernists admired: aimless joy, sensual diversion, mere decoration. As early as 1963 Lionel Trilling suggested that the modernist revolution had succeeded too well; it made intelligent audiences love what is hard and what is "good" for them at the expense of what really gives them pleasure.[10]

4

Henri Matisse once wrote: "What I dream of is an art of balance, purity, and serenity, without troubling or depressing subject matter, an art that gives any intellectual worker (a businessman and writer, for example) some peace of mind, rather as a good armchair gives him rest from physical labor."[11] Matisse not only imagined such a happy art, he was our century's greatest creator of it.

Among the major creators of the second rank was Paul Manship, who, feeling mortal, wrote in 1943, "I am always fearful that the old reputation will slump."[12] Slump it did, but with the current vogue of ornamentalism and of "art as fun," it is rising again; prices for his work have started up. On his hundredth birthday Manship can sleep easy. Reputation is fickle, but competent sculpture has a long half-life; his time has been and gone, and is coming.

William M. Stott
Professor of American Studies and English
Director, American Studies Programs
The University of Texas at Austin

Notes

1

John B. Vickery, *The Literary Impact of "The Golden Bough,"* (Princeton: Princeton University Press, 1973), 33. For a view of the upper class art audience in America in the late nineteenth century, see John Tomsich, *A Genteel Endeavor: American Culture and Politics in The Gilded Age* (Stanford: Stanford University Press, 1971).

2

Paul Manship, 18 February 1959, interview with John D. Morse; quoted in Frederick D. Leach, introduction to *Paul Howard Manship: An Intimate View* (Saint Paul: Minnesota Museum of Art, 1972), 16. Leach's introduction is the best overview we have of Manship's life.

3

Paul Manship, 4 December 1915, speech to the Art Students' League of New York City; quoted in Leach, 19.

4

Paul Manship, October 1937 talk at the University of Iowa; quoted in Leach, 16.

5

Paul Manship, May 1912 speech to the American Academy in Rome; quoted in Edwin Murtha, *Paul Manship,* (New York: Macmillan, 1957), 12. This handsomely printed book has the best and largest collection of photographs of Manship's work.

6

Royal Cortissoz, review in *The New York Herald Tribune,* 15 April 1933; quoted in Leach, 34.

7

Jeffrey L. Meikle, *Twentieth Century Limited: Industrial Design in America, 1925-1939* (Philadelphia: Temple University Press, 1979). On this theme, see also my articles "Greenbelt and Futurama: The Heavenly Cities of the 1930s," *Journal of the American Studies Association of Texas* (1973), 18-29; and "Hard Times and Happy Days: The Visual Iconography of Depression America," in a forthcoming volume of the proceedings of the 1982-83 Lowell Conference on Industrial History, published by the Museum of American Textile History. I am grateful to Jeff Meikle for counsel he has given me on this article. I am grateful also to these other colleagues for help they have given: Janice Bradley, John Clarke, Robert Crunden, Carol Mundorff and Jennifer Scalora.

8

William Jordy, *The Impact of European Modernism in the Mid-Twentieth Century,* vol. 4 of his *American Buildings and Their Architects* (Garden City: Anchor Press/Doubleday, 1976), 16, 75.

9

I discuss this theme briefly in my book *Documentary Expression and Thirties America* (New York: Oxford University Press, 1973), 53-55.

10

Lionel Trilling, "The Fate of Pleasure," *Partisan Review,* 1963; reprinted in his *Beyond Culture: Essays on Literature and Learning* (New York: Viking Press, 1965), 57-87. On this theme, see also Irving Howe, "Books," *Harper's Magazine* (May 1971), 102-10.

11

Henri Matisse, from an essay in *La Grande Revue,* 25 December 1908, as quoted in Lewis Aragon, *Henri Matisse: A Novel,* trans. Jean Stewart (New York: Harcourt Brace Jovanovich, 1972), vol. 2, 284-85. There is another version of the statement in the Howe article.

12

Paul Manship, 13 May 1943, letter to Booth Tarkington, quoted in Leach, 31.

89. *Cycle of Life — Armillary Sphere,*
1920-1937
bronze
28 x 24⅜ x 31½
66.14.35
Murtha 364

An armillary sphere is an ancient astronomical device illustrating the relationship among the great circles of the heavens. Manship's sphere consists of four rings and a diagonal axis which is located inside the sphere. Personifications of the twelve signs of the zodiac ornament the outer side of the widest band of the sphere. On one of the narrow bands, the names of the signs are inscribed. The other two bands bear decorative motifs symbolizing the elements. The North Star is positioned outside the sphere, on the tip of the central axis, flanked by two griffins, part eagle and part lion. A family group entitled "Cycle of Life" is placed inside the skeletal sphere, at the base. The sphere was described by Manship as symbolizing the "Cycle of Eternity," and the turtles which support the sphere as "emblems of eternity." (Murtha 111)

Designed as a sundial, the shadow from the central axis is projected onto the inner part of the widest band of the sphere. Roman numerals are engraved on the interior of this band, indicating the time of day where the shadow rests.

Manship made several versions of the *Cycle of Life — Armillary Sphere.* The first version was completed in 1918 and was also called *Humanity and Eternity.* The second version was finished in 1920 and was enlarged as a garden sculpture several times. One of these versions is located in

Brookgreen Gardens. MMA owns a third version of the sphere, completed in 1937, which differs from the earlier versions in the simplification of the bands. The outermost rim is not ornamented by projecting flames and the bronze base lacks the wave motif. The zodiacs are in high rather than low relief, as in earlier versions.

S.L.

Fig. 20
*Woodrow Wilson Memorial — Celestial
Sphere,* 1939
bronze with gilded constellations and
silvered stars
25' high
Palais des Nations,
Geneva, Switzerland
Murtha 399

The *Celestial Sphere* was given by a private
American Society — the Woodrow Wilson
Foundation.

The gift, presented in 1939, is in
memory of President Wilson, founder of
the League of Nations.

The sphere is of bronze, and was
designed by the American sculptor Paul
Manship. It represents the signs of the
zodiac and was cast and finished in Italy by
Bruno Bearzi.

The sphere is situated in the Court of
Honor of the Palais des Nations, facing the
Assembly Building. It rotates in the same
direction as the earth and is inclined at the
same angle.

reprinted with permission of
the Office of Public Information
United Nations
Palais des Nations
Geneva, Switzerland

90. *Capricorn,* n.d.
terra-cotta
17 x 26 x 5⅛
66.14.65j

This terra-cotta figure, one of twelve
owned by MMA, (66.14.65a-l), may have
been a study for the final bronze version
for the *Armillary Sphere and Sundial* (Fig.
21) at the 1964-1965 New York World's
Fair (destroyed). This sphere featured a
zodiacal band, as did his earlier armillary
spheres. The zodiac figures on this band
were cast in high relief in bronze and gold
as individual sculptures.

  Manship illustrated Capricorn, the
tenth astrological sign of the zodiac in the
traditional manner — as a sea-goat with
the head and forequarters of a goat and the
sinuous body and curled, spiraling tail of
a fish.
L.A.K.
S.L.

Fig. 21
Armillary Sphere and Sundial, 1964
bronze, partially gilded, granite base
c. 12′ diameter
1964-1965
New York World's Fair
(destroyed)

Manship's last armillary sphere was
commissioned by the New York World's
Fair Corporation art committee. The fact
that Manship was one of four finalists
chosen to create a monumental sculpture
for the Fair is evidence of his continued
popularity.

  Described as one of his largest and
most important commissions, Manship's
sphere is bronze, and the central figure
group is gilded. Unlike Manship's earlier
armillary sphere which includes the Cycle
of Life group in the center, figures of an
elderly man and a child, symbolizing the
passage of time, are incorporated in the
1964 sphere.
S.L.

91. *Male Centaur and Female Satyr,* n.d.
ink on paper
6½ x 7½
66.14.140a

92. *Female Satyr Riding on Back of Male Centaur,* n.d.
ink on paper
5¾ x 7¼
66.14.140b

93. *Male Centaur Holding Baby Satyr,* n.d.
ink on paper
7¾ x 5⅝
66.14.140c

These drawings were studies for three designs on the Steuben glass vase designed by Manship. These undoubtedly were the original drawings from which the Steuben Glass engraver worked.

The drawings tell a story of the courting of a female satyr by a male centaur. The drawing on the left depicts courtship: the satyr holds a bouquet of flowers given to her by the posturing centaur. In the center drawing, the satyr rides on the centaur's back; his hands grasp her waist protectively. A rabbit, symbolizing fertility, sits amid flowers, looking up at the couple. In the drawing

on the right, the centaur joyously holds up a baby satyr, a gift of their love.

In these drawings, the artist used his imagination to create a story featuring mythological characters in untraditional roles. Very seldom are satyrs and centaurs shown as lovers, and female satyrs are rare in classical art. In Italian Renaissance art, for example, satyr families were portrayed in the bronze statuettes of Riccio.
L.A.K.
S.L.

94. *Steuben Vase, 1938-1940   4/6*
crystal, clear glass, hand-wheel engraved
14 x 8½ x 5½
Collection The Art Institute of Chicago
Gift of Mrs. William H. Stanley
1961.248
Murtha 391

In 1937, the Director of Steuben Glass,
John M. Gates, was inspired by Henri
Matisse to gather the "greatest
contemporary artists in Europe and
America"* to create designs to be engraved
in crystal. Paul Manship was asked to
submit drawings. Other participants
included Georgia O'Keeffe, Aristide
Maillol, Isamu Noguchi, Raoul Dufy and
Salvadore Dali. The final works were
displayed in the exhibition entitled
"Twenty-Seven Contemporary Artists in
Crystal" on view in New York from
10 January-14 February 1940.
    The process of converting drawing to
glass is described as follows:
    *Working from the designer's drawings, the
Steuben Glass engraver first coats the glass with
protective shellac, then transfers the image onto
the surface with India ink.***
    Paul Manship's vase was greatly
admired by Frank Jewett Mather, Jr., the
Director and Curator of the Museum of
Historic Art at Princeton University, who
wrote the preface to the catalogue
accompanying the 1940 Steuben Glass
exhibition. He noted that Manship, along
with Dufy, were the only two artists who
decorated most of the surface of the vase,
rather than just one small part "using the
transparency instead of ignoring it." He
adds:
    It seems to me that Manship of all the

*contributors has most fully realized that he was
dealing with a new problem and must find a
new idiom in order to solve it, and while I by
no means deprecate other more conventional
methods, I am ready to guess that the historian
of intaglio design in transparent glass is likely
to award pioneer honor to Mr. Manship.****
    Manship's intaglio designs on the
Steuben vase are stylistically similar to
what he was striving for in his sculpture at

this time; the vase designs are to be viewed
primarily as graceful silhouettes.
Designs in Glass by 27 Contemporary Artists
(New York: Steuben Glass, Inc., 1940),
unpaginated brochure.
**Mary J. Madigan, *Steuben Glass, An
American Tradition in Crystal* (New York:
Steuben Glass, Inc., 1982), 45.
***Designs in Glass.*
S.L.

Paul Manship: A Biographical Sketch

95. *Indian Hunter and His Dog.* 1926
bronze, marble base
22⅓ x 23 x 8½
Collection Minnesota Museum of Art
Gift of Mrs. Arthur H. Savage
65.04.01
Murtha 199

This sculpture depicts an Indian youth with a dog at his side and is a bronze study for a life-size grouping of figures designed to stand in a pool. Commissioned by Thomas Cochran, Jr., in memory of his father, a prominent Saint Paul businessman, the life-size sculpture was placed in Cochran Memorial Park at Western and Summit Avenues. Because of vandalism, the sculpture was removed from Cochran Memorial Park in 1967 and installed outside the Como Park Conservatory. In 1983 a fiberglas facsimile was installed in its place in Cochran Park by the City of Saint Paul.

The boy races along, his bow grasped in his left hand, two arrows held in his right. Two feathers flutter from his top-knot. A dog runs alongside his master, with a lion-like mane covering his neck and shoulders. His head is up, ears curled back, mouth slightly open. *Indian Hunter* is surrounded by four Canadian geese whose necks arch back to form the fountain.

The drawing for *Indian Hunter and His Dog* has the same sense of speed as the final bronze sculpture. No arrows appear in the sketch and the treatment of the hair and breechcloth have changed slightly from the drawing to the bronze sketch.

Manship depicts the Indian as a youth rather than as a mature man, as in *Indian*

When I was a child in the 1930s, my father Paul Manship was at the height of his career and of his celebrity. We lived a good life; we children attended private schools and my mother had servants to help her in the town house in which we lived in Manhattan, one of five that my father had bought in the mid-1920s. He maintained two studios, one in Paris and one in New York, and both were buzzing with activity. He employed a number of assistants (some were to become well-known — Henry Kreis, Albert Stewart and Carl Schmitz in particular), as there was a lot of work to be done in realizing a number of major commissions. These included the youthful Lincoln for Fort Wayne, Indiana 1932, the Paul Rainey Memorial Gates for the New York Zoological Park (Fig. 11) 1934, the famous gilded *Prometheus,* 1934, for Rockefeller Center in New York (Fig. 16), the Woodrow Wilson Memorial Celestial Sphere for the League of Nations in Geneva (Fig. 20) 1939, and the sculptures for the New York World's Fair of 1939 — *Time and the Fates Sundial* (80) and the four *Moods of Time* (82-87) — as well as the usual complement of portraits, medals, tablets and small bronzes. His only rivals in the United States were James Earle Fraser and Lee Lawrie, both of whom were older men specializing in public commissions. Internationally his peers were Carl Milles and Ivan Mestrovic.

Despite the depression this was a period of considerable activity in sculpture. The revolution in taste that occurred in the 1950s has led historians and critics to slight this period. Only now as another change of taste is taking place is an effort being made to study and to give credit to the artists of this time, and particularly among American sculptors to Paul Manship.

He was born in Saint Paul, Minnesota, on Christmas Eve, 1885. He was the seventh child of a former Confederate soldier from Mississippi, who had gone North after the Civil War to seek opportunities unavailable in the defeated South. Paul's mother, Mary Etta Friend, was a Minnesota pioneer, whose father had originally come from Maryland. His grandfather, Charles Manship, was something of a tastemaker in Jackson, Mississippi. He had been trained as an ornamental painter, doing graining and stencil work, in his home state of Maryland and had gone to Jackson when Mississippi was admitted to the Union to work on the new

(97) 1914. The running form of the youth lends itself to the streamlining introduced in the work. Manship has employed a classical touch in the naturalistic modeling of the work.

Manship stated many times, to life-long friend Ben Storey, Sr., and to Saint Paul columnist Gareth Hiebert, "Oliver Towne," that *Indian Hunter and His Dog* was his favorite sculpture, because it reminded him of his boyhood in Saint Paul.

J.F.H.

Fig. 22
Paul Manship, Archival Photograph

Governor's Mansion and the State Capitol. He was mayor of Jackson during the Civil War; he had an interior design business, and after the war he built for his family an interesting Gothic house, which is now restored and open to the public. It has been designated a National Landmark, and is a show place in Jackson. Paul's older brother Luther was a painter; he taught art in the public schools and painted landscapes in an academic impressionist style. Another brother, Albert, was a poet. Luther unfortunately was crippled with asthma. With Paul's financial help he spent his last years in the Southwest, where the desert environment made it possible for him to breathe and paint. Paul also suffered from asthma, although not so severely as Luther, but all his life it curtailed his activity and made country living impossible for him.

Art was thus a factor in the Manship home, and it was also a factor in Saint Paul at the turn of the century. Culture had been introduced to the area through the person of August Jaccaci, who was employed as a tutor to the family of James J. Hill and guided Hill in developing his private collection of European paintings. He was a friend of young Paul, as was the painter Nathaniel Poussette-Dart, a contemporary and school chum. If Paul was interested in art from a fairly early age, he had more normal boyish interests as well. The Manships had a cabin on Bald Eagle Lake, where they went in the summers. There Paul developed a life-long taste for hunting and fishing and an interest in animals, which was to surface when he did the Rainey Gates.

He studied art at the Saint Paul Institute, concentrating first on painting, but the discovery that he was color-blind led him to transfer his interest to modeling. He left school at the age of seventeen, and for a short time he had his own design business. He did sign painting and lettering — and in fact lettering was to remain a life-long interest of his. Soon, however, he was to go East to pursue his studies. In New York he studied at the Arts Students' League with George Bridgman, the celebrated teacher of artistic anatomy, and then at the Pennsylvania Academy of the Fine Arts with Charles Grafly; but the most important influence on him at this time was that of the great Western sculptor Solon Borglum, for whom he worked as an assistant. Borglum was at that time at work on his *Rough-Rider* Monument, and Paul for the rest of his life had the ambition

96. *Study for Indian Hunter and His Dog,*
n.d.
crayon and pencil on paper
24½ x 25⅛
66.14.200

Fig. 23
Indian Hunter and His Dog, 1926
Cochran Memorial Park, Saint Paul; this
original sculpture was moved to the Como
Park Conservatory, Saint Paul, 1967.

to create his own equestrian monument, an ambition which was to be
frustrated by adverse circumstances. He later worked for the Viennese-
American sculptor Isidore Konti. It was Konti who urged him to apply to
the American Academy in Rome. In 1909 he won a scholarship to Rome
and stayed there for three years. He was twenty-three years old.

My father frequently spoke of what a difference it made to his art that
he went to Rome at this sensitive moment in his life, rather than to Paris.
Paris, the seat of the Académie des Beaux-Arts, was where the American
sculptors of the older generation had studied — Saint-Gaudens, French,
MacMonnies and Borglum; at this time it was most significantly the home
of Rodin, the greatest and most celebrated sculptor of his time. Young
sculptors who came close to him were profoundly influenced by him. But
Paul Manship escaped Rodin's influence and instead, in Rome and Greece,
came under that of the classical sculptors, particularly the masters of
archaic Greece.

97. *Indian,* 1914
bronze, marble base
14½ x 13⁵/₁₆ x 8½
National Museum of American Art,
Smithsonian Institution
Gift of Paul Manship
1965.16.14
Murtha 51

These sculptures form a pair. The Indian
hunter kneels on his right knee, his right
arm drawn back in the act of releasing an
arrow, his left arm extended, a bow
grasped in his hand. An animal skin lies
folded over his left thigh.

The antelope rears back on its hind legs
in pained surprise, its side pierced by an
arrow. The stylized details on the stricken
animal's body are simplified and daintily
modeled. Manship has transformed
naturalistic features into decorative
elements in his treatment of the head and
neck areas.

Although *Indian* is realistically
modeled, Manship imparts a suggestion of
archaic Greek sculpture in the pose of the
figure.
J.F.H.

His three-year stay at the Academy in Rome saw the formation of Paul
Manship's distinctive style. It was based on an eclectic amalgam of
influences. If nature as he had learned to handle it through his studies
with the Beaux-Arts-trained sculptors Grafly and Borglum, was the basis,
it became nature stylized and refined into a very personal art. This
stylization owes much to his deep love for the sculptures of archaic Greece,
medieval France, Renaissance Italy, China and India. He came freshly to
these sources, but others among his contemporaries were also influenced
by them — Bourdelle and Milles by ancient Greece, Mestrovic and Eric
Gill by Romanesque art. It was a time that a high stylishness was in the
air. Art Nouveau was giving way to Art Deco. John Canaday has written
scornfully of bookends as characteristic of this period; what is
characteristic of it is a desire to make everything into art, as Bugatti did
with the automobile, Fortuny with textiles, Poiret and Chanel with
women's clothing, and Tiffany with everything he touched. In this spirit
Manship was to make lamps and candlesticks, windowboxes, furniture,
ashtrays, vases, a balcony railing, a drinking fountain — but no bookends.

98. *Pronghorn Antelope*, 1914
bronze, marble base
13⁹/₁₆″ x 10⅜″ x 8½″
National Museum of American Art,
Smithsonian Institution
Gift of Paul Manship
1965.16.15
Murtha 52

Manship's style was at the opposite extreme from Rodin's
Impressionism. Every form was considered and perfected, polished almost
like jewelry. This concern with the purity of form represented a radical
break with the dominant Beaux Arts style. In Beaux Arts sculpture every
accident of modeling is carefully preserved in the final bronze; in
Manship's work these are deliberately eliminated. He achieved this by
extensively working inside the mold and by working over the plaster
model. With the hindsight of a quarter of a century, I see a greater
likeness between Manship's work and that of Archipenko, Zadkine and
even Brancusi — despite their tendencies toward abstraction — than
between Manship's and that of such Expressionist descendants of Rodin as
Epstein and Lipchitz.

Paul Manship came back to New York in 1912 with the sculptures he
had done in Rome. On 1 January 1913, he married Isabel McIlwaine,
whom he had met seven years earlier at Solon Borglum's house in
Silvermine. Their marriage was to last happily until his death more than
fifty-three years later. The next few years were triumphant; his first

99. *Briseis,* 1916
gilded bronze
23 high
Collection Mr. and Mrs. Gerald P. Peters
Murtha 88

exhibitions were huge successes and a shock of excitement was felt among art lovers because of the novelty and originality of the work. Museum shows followed in Chicago, St. Louis, Cincinnati, Detroit and Buffalo — and his work was acquired for their permanent collections. He had his first commissions from architects — from Grant La Farge for a marble St. Joseph in the Blessed Sacrament Church in Providence, Rhode Island, 1913; from Welles Bosworth for a number of sculptures for the American Telephone and Telegraph Company building on Broadway at Fulton Street, 1914; and from Charles Platt for many garden sculptures. So began a fruitful period of collaboration with architects. Bosworth (who outlived Manship by a few months, dying at the age of ninety-eight) and Platt (who served as my godfather) remained close friends. Later there were others — Thomas Ellett, John Harbison and especially Eric Gugler, who for forty years was Manship's closest friend and collaborator; he was the architect for his houses in New York and in Gloucester, and collaborated on the Anzio and Roosevelt commissions.

At this time Manship began to do portraits, and did some important ones, including the head of John Barrymore, 1918, the marble bust of John D. Rockefeller, 1918, and the elaborately framed portrait of his infant daughter Pauline Frances (105) 1914. The latter represents the highpoint of Renaissance influence on his work. It was acquired early by The Metropolitan Museum of Art, as was the *Centaur and Dryad* (42) 1913. The Metropolitan commissioned the memorial of John Pierpont Morgan, on which he worked from 1915 to 1920. In his busy studio he required assistants to help him in all this work. These included three men who were later to become famous in their own right — Gaston Lachaise, Benjamin Bufano and Reuben Nakian.

When the United States entered the First World War, Paul Manship volunteered to serve with the Red Cross in Italy. After the war, his career continued its successful course. During the 1920s he lived mainly in Europe with his growing family. They lived first in London as guests of John Singer Sargent, who helped him procure important commissions, among which was the marble portrait of Lady Cholmondeley, 1923. In Paris, he set up a studio on the Rue du Val de Grace, which he kept until 1937, when the rumors of impending war led him to give it up. Two of

138

100. *Briseis*, 1950
marble, marble base
29¾ x 9½ x 7
66.14.105
Murtha 513

Manship's *Briseis* sculptures of 1916 and 1950 embody the full classical mode of expression, with their emphasis on proportion and harmony, the basic ideals of Greek art. Both sensitively-stylized forms show Manship's predilection for returning to favorite themes over the years, often reworking them in subtle new ways.

Agamemnon, leader of the Greek armies, had won a priest's daughter as a prize of war. On the advice of a seer he relinquished her, and laid claim to the slave-girl, *Briseis,* property of Achilles. Both men fought over her, but Agamemnon won. Manship portrays her as she is being led away, her head lowered, and handed over to Agamemnon. In the myth she looks yearningly back at Achilles.

It is interesting to note that the 1950 version is one of few examples where Manship employed the fragment idea — *Briseis* is armless and her figure cut off at the thighs — an approach which Rodin espoused. In both works, the incisions are subtle, though different materials are used. The white marble adds to the gentle melancholy mood of the work, showing Manship's sensitivity to materials. The 1916 full figure of *Briseis* in bronze was possibly made for a garden; she stands delicately poised on a round pedestal with long, billowing drapery over her arms. MMA owns a plaster study of a 1916 *Briseis*, (66.14.106).
G.K.

his daughters were born in Paris during this period — Elizabeth in 1921 and Sarah Janet in 1929. I, however, was born in 1927 in New York in the newly-acquired house on East 72nd Street. My mother claimed that she was certain she was going to have a boy and didn't want him to run the danger of having to serve in the French army.

During these years Manship produced the works for which he is especially well known. These include *Flight of Night* (44) 1916, *Dancer and Gazelles* (40) 1916, the armillary sphere called the *Cycle of Life* (89) 1920, *Atalanta* (Fig. 67) 1921, *Diana* (45) 1921 and *Actaeon* (46) 1923, *Europa and the Bull* (14) 1924, the *Flight of Europa* (15) 1925, and the *Indian Hunter and his Dog* (95) 1926. Honors were showered on him. In 1916 he was elected to the National Academy of Design as an Academician, in

Fig. 24
Manship's studio and home in Lanesville,
near Gloucester, Massachusettes

Fig. 25
Manship's living room, East 72nd Street,
New York City

Fig. 26
Manship family portrait, from left to
right, Sarah Janet, Isabel Manship, John,
Paul Manship, Elizabeth and Pauline, New
York City

Fig. 27
Gari Melchers (1860-1932)
Paul Manship, 1932
oil on canvas
19 x 15
Collection Century Association, New York
Gift of the Estate of Paul Manship

Gari Melchers was a painter of portraits
and scenes in the impressionist style. This
portrait of Paul Manship is an idealized
depiction of the sculptor at the height of
his career. Manship appears as an
intellectual in his formal attire rather than
the typical artist with tools in hand.

Manship also made two portraits of
Gari Melchers in 1932; these bronze and
plaster medallion portraits (Murtha 301)
are in the collection of the Century
Association, New York.
S.L.

1920 to the National Institute of Arts and Letters, in 1932 to the
American Academy of Arts and Letters (of which he was later to be
President), and in 1929 he became a *chevalier de la Légion d'honneur.* He was
named a corresponding member of a number of foreign academies as well,
including the Académie des Beaux-Arts in Paris, the Accademia di San
Luca in Rome, and the Argentine National Academy. In 1935, through
the good offices of his friend, the art dealer, Sir Joseph Duveen, he was
invited to exhibit his work at the Tate Gallery in London...with the
exception of Rodin, he was the only living foreign sculptor to be so
honored at that time.

If I as a child in the 1930s didn't experience the hard times felt by so
many of my friends, the 1940s were different — not hard times exactly
but a tightened belt. During the Second World War, there was no
sculpture being done. The foundries were doing war work and no metal
was available for casting. We moved from a town house to an apartment in
the building next door that my father also owned. The family was
shrinking; Pauline married, Elizabeth volunteered to serve with the WACs
in the South Pacific. To keep his hand in, Manship did portraits in terra-
cotta of his friends. To earn extra money he took to the lecture circuit, and
it was at this time that he took a position teaching at the Pennsylvania
Academy of Fine Arts in Philadelphia. It was also during these years that
he bought the quarries in Gloucester, Massachusetts, where he built his
summer home and studio and planned his gardens with the architectural
advice of his friend Eric Gugler.

When the war was over, it was clear that we were living in a different
world. Modernism had been introduced early from Europe — we usually
cite the New York Armory Show as its American debut — and for thirty
years it had been making inroads in the American art scene. After the war
it conquered outright. Paul Manship was lucky. If he lost the adulation of
the critics and his accepted status as America's leading sculptor (this title
would then probably have been bestowed on Alexander Calder or David
Smith), he had a succession of important commissions that were to keep
him occupied until his death. He now worked wholly at commissions or
for his own pleasure, and eschewed the unfriendly gallery scene. Among
these jobs were the statue of John Hancock in Boston, 1948, the

101. *Study for Balcony Railing,* n.d.
pencil on paper
9⅞ x 13⅜
66.14.141C
cf. Murtha 200

Manship designed a wrought iron and
gilded bronze railing for his New York
City townhouse in 1926, which was placed
on a balcony overlooking the dining room.
This drawing is closely related to the
finished work (Fig. 28).

The balcony railing is divided into
three panels. On the left and right panels,
a nude man and woman recline, supported
by stylized cloud forms. In the drawing a
child is seated in the central panel. In the
final work, the child is represented
standing.

Four posts rest on top of the railing.
These twisting supports are surmounted
by sculptures of dancing children. MMA
owns casts of three of these little dancers,
two of which have been alternately titled
by Murtha *Charleston 1* (66.14.11a) and
Charleston 11 (66.14.78, Murtha 203).
S.L.

Fig. 28
Manship's dining room, East 72nd Street,
New York City

143

102. *John Manship*, 1932
terra cotta, wood base
14 x 7 x 8
66.14.25
cf. Murtha 300

Paul Manship's only son is shown here at
the age of six. He was named after John
Singer Sargent, Manship's good friend and
colleague. It was Sargent who mentioned
to John D. Rockefeller that Manship had a
"fine head" for sculpture. That 1918 bust
of John D. Rockefeller was the first of
many portrait commissions to follow.
Sargent also made a quick sketch of
Manship smoking and straddling his chair
which is in the collection of The
Metropolitan Museum of Art, and
illustrated in MMA's 1972 catalogue *Paul
Howard Manship: An Intimate View*.
Another version, of *John Manship*, in
porcelain, is in MMA's collection
(66.14.50).
G.K.

sculptures for the military cemetery in Anzio, 1952-1954, the Osborn,
1952 and Lehman, 1957, Gates for Central Park in New York (Figs. 12,
13), the Armillary Sphere for the New York World's Fair of 1964 (Fig.
21), and the monumental portrait statue of Theodore Roosevelt in
Washington, 1967. Other sculptors we knew fared much worse —
Nadelman, who committed suicide, Edward McCartan, who died in
penury, John Gregory, who was inactive because of lack of interest in his
art, and Leo Lentelli, who spent his last years in Rome living off a meager
Social Security check that went farther there than it would have in the
States.

Paul Manship's old age was on the whole a happy and productive time,
despite his being attacked or, worse yet, ignored by the critics, and his
being cited as a Communist by the House un-American Activities
Committee, a ridiculous charge which was inspired by his membership in
the 1930s in the American Artists Congress, his friendships with Hugo
Gellert and Rockwell Kent, and his public stands against the rise of
Fascism. The family spent time together at the quarries in Gloucester and
in Italy, where Sarah Jane and her husband Edwin, and my wife Margaret
and I were living. His son-in-law Edwin Murtha catalogued his work and
was the author of the book *Paul Manship*, published by Macmillan in
1957. His daughter-in-law, the sculptor Margaret Cassidy, helped out in
the studio, assisting especially in the final work, which was done in Paris
in 1964, on the *Theodore Roosevelt Monument*.

Manship's creative powers remained as strong as ever. These years saw
the creation of two exceptionally fine marble sculptures of women, the
Susanna, 1948 and the *Leda*, 1955. In 1960 he was asked to do the
inaugural medal for John F. Kennedy, as he had done for Franklin
Roosevelt (114) in 1932. It was also during these last two decades of his
life that he produced most of the marvellous little mythological groups,
which he modeled directly in wax and which were cast as unique bronzes
by the *cire perdu* technique.

He died suddenly in his New York apartment at the National Arts
Club, while preparing breakfast, in January of 1966, a month after his
eightieth birthday. He had returned only a short time before from Italy,
where he had spent Christmas with Isabel, who was staying with Sarah

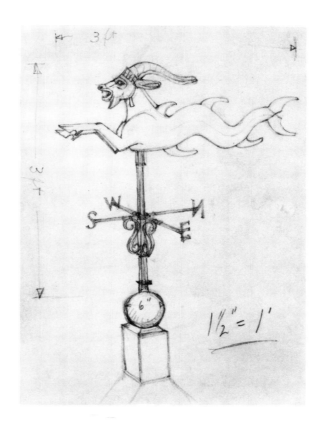

103. *Study for Capricorn Weathervane*, n.d.
pencil on paper
7½ x 5¼
66.14.131c

104. *Jonah and the Whale Weathervane*, n.d.
ink on vellum
13 x 16⅜
Augsburg College Permanent Collection
Gift of Mr. and Mrs. Donald G. Padilla

The only known weathervane that Manship
executed in sculpture was the copper
Sagittarius Weathervane, completed in 1948
for his Gloucester, Massachusetts studio
(Fig. 24, Murtha 501). The drawing of
the Capricorn weathervane may have been
a study for the copper version since both
have similar bases (three-dimensional
rectangular shapes topped by globes).

Another drawing of a weathervane, in
the collection of Augsburg College,
illustrates the biblical tale of *Jonah and the
Whale*. The nude figure of Jonah is
illustrated in a classical pose of either
being swallowed by or expelled from the
mouth of a large whimsical whale.

Whale weathervanes were common
ornaments in whaling towns along the
Atlantic coast and the drawing of the
Jonah and the Whale Weathervane may have
been done with New England seacoast
patrons in mind.
S.L.

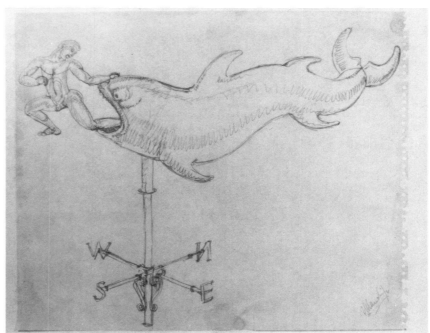

105. *Pauline Frances*, 1914
polychromed plaster
21 x 12⅛ x 5⅛
66.14.48
Murtha 35

This is the plaster version of a portrait of
Manship's first child at the age of three
weeks. Although the little face has the old-
as-time-look of all young infants, Pauline
is not an idealized or sentimentalized
infant but portrayed realistically. It was
rare that a portrait be done of so young a
child. The wrapped infant is placed in a
rounded niche and surrounded by a border.
Putti with garlands ornament the front of
the base while long-legged storks are
depicted on each side.

 The final, more ornate marble version
is in the collection of The Metropolitan
Museum of Art (Murtha 34) and has an
elaborate border and lavishly decorated
niche. The influence of Italian Renaissance
art is evident in this work and recalls
works by Donatello and Luca Della
Robbia.
J.F.H.

106. *Portrait of Isabel McIlwaine*, 1912
oil on board
7½ x 5½
Collection Mr. and Mrs. John Manship

107. *Self Portrait*, 1912
oil on board
10⅛ x 6⅜
Collection Mr. and Mrs. John Manship

Jane and her family, and where he had gone to see the casting of the
Roosevelt statue into bronze. His final major project, unfortunately
aborted by his death, was for a pair of monumental groups for the east
front of the Capitol. We received the plaster scale model of one of these
from the casters in Rome after his death. The groups were to have
portrayed the seventeenth century settlers of the original colonies and the
nineteenth century pioneers of the West — honoring, in a way, his own
forebears. Plaster models of these have been on view in the lower rotunda
of the Capitol. In his will he left the bronzes and other completed work in
his two studios (New York and Gloucester) to be divided between two
museums, the Saint Paul Art Center and the National Collection of Fine
Arts (as they were then called). The latter he had a hand in establishing in
its splendid home in the old Patent Office, when he was Chairman of the
Smithsonian Art Commission.

 With his death his reputation went into limbo. We sensed this almost
at once. At the dedication of the Roosevelt Monument in 1967, none of
the dignitaries present, from the President to the Chief Justice, from the

Paintings by Manship are rare; *Self Portrait* and *Portrait of Isabel McIlwaIne*, whom he was courting and had met earlier at the Solon Borglum home, are among the few works Manship executed in this medium.

Manship later gave up painting on discovering he was color-blind and turned his energies totally to sculpture.

These works reflect Manship's study with Charles Grafly at the Pennsylvania Academy of Fine Arts, whose specialty was portraiture. Manship captured the direct and straightforward style of his master, eliminating unnecessary details; yet the works are painterly, textured and individualized.

G.K.

Secretary of the Interior to the surviving children of Theodore Roosevelt, mentioned Paul Manship's name as creator of the statue. The Washington Post made up for this with a tirade on his conservatism and classicism, attacking him as well for the Rayburn Office Building. His only connection with that project had been a marble portrait bust of the Speaker of the House.

Almost twenty years have passed since Paul Manship's death and once again the artistic climate is changing. His work is again widely admired. In sixty years of creative life he produced a large body of work, including a number of public monuments, a large group of exceptionally fine decorative bronzes and marbles. This group includes portraits, sculptures of animals, many unique small bronzes, the functional objects I have already listed, garden sculptures, medals, designs for stamps and coinage and memorial tablets. He also produced a few paintings, and a large number of drawings.

In an article for a memorial show in the early 1970s, I compared my father's role in the art of his time with that of Ingres almost exactly a century earlier. Like Ingres, he emerged as something of a revolutionary, and while changing relatively little over a long life, ended as an arch-conservative. Like Ingres he wanted to establish a monument to his art and his ideals; Saint Paul was to be his Montaubon. As craftsmen, both were perfectionists. Both were self-consciously classicists and both were defenders of classical standards against what each considered to be a wave of barbarism; but their classicism was tempered by a degree of sensuality. Both admired the beauty of women. Over his long life, Paul Manship gradually purged his work of the eclectic influences of his beginnings. His later sculpture was both more realistic and more classical than the earlier. He once mentioned a problem that he had. In every woman's body the spinal column is evident in the lower back but it is never indicated by the Greek sculptors. Should he therefore follow the example of nature or that of the Greeks? He chose the Greeks. One of the advantages of classicism is that its ideal is outside of time and of fashion; the artist who serves it can therefore never be really out of date.

John Manship

108. *Pyrma Tilton*, 1927
plaster, gilded wood frame
12⅝ diameter
66.14.55
Murtha 227

Pyrma Tilton was the stepdaughter of
Herbert Claiborne Pell (1885-1961), a
congressman and a diplomat; both Pell and
Manship were friends of Franklin Delano
Roosevelt. Pyrma Tilton is portrayed as a
fashionable young woman of the 1920s
with hair neatly bobbed just over the ears,
wearing two strands of pearls around her
neck. The portrait may have been a
wedding present for the young woman's
mother, Olive Bigelow, who married
Herbert Pell in Paris the same year as the

portrait was completed. Olive Pell was a
painter especially appreciated by
contemporaries for her portraits, and a
sculpted portrait of her daughter by the
popular artist Paul Manship would
undoubtedly have been received with
delight. Paul Manship created several
portrait medallions in 1927, including the
portrait of Ann Rainey. These were
executed in terra-cotta, and depict the
subject's head in profile against a circular
background. *Pyrma Tilton* is in plaster, and
is likely a cast of the original terra-cotta.

Unlike Manship's other portrait
medallions, the profile of *Pyrma Tilton* is
framed with flowers.
S.L.

Fig. 29
Triple Portrait Relief, 1956
gilded bronze, red Alicante marble
32½ x 32½
Courtesy 3M, Saint Paul
Murtha 574

In late 1955 or early 1956, Manship was commissioned to execute a memorial for the Minnesota Mining and Manufacturing Company. The memorial consists of three gilded bronze profile portraits of the company's founders. Their names are written on the banners beneath, from left to right: William L. McKnight, Archibald G. Bush and Richard P. Carlton. The dedication is inscribed on a rectangular plaque below the portraits and both works are mounted on marble.

In creating the portraits, Manship worked partially from photographs; Carlton had died before the memorial was begun and Bush was in poor health. McKnight visited him in his New York studio, and Manship was able to complete his features from life.

This memorial installed at 3M's Central Research Building, is significant in that it is one of the two commissioned works on display in Manship's native city. The other work in Saint Paul is the life-size bronze *Indian Hunter and His Dog* fountain in Como Park.
J.F.H.
S.L.

Fig. 30
Paul Manship and W. L. McKnight in Manship's New York studio, late 1955 or early 1956

MEDALS

Paul Manship designed hundreds of medals during his lifetime commemorating persons or events. The history of the medal goes back to ancient times, when medals were struck for prizes in games or significant events. The Romans made many in gold, silver, brass or copper. In modern times, medals were often used to represent or illustrate history. In America, medals were presented as awards during the revolutionary period, but following the War of 1812 medals became somewhat unfashionable. The practice was revived during the Civil War to commemorate great men, and has continued ever since, primarily through commissions of philanthropists and presidents such as Rockefeller, Roosevelt and Kennedy.

Although Manship's imagery was derived from Greek mythology and art, the format and design were influenced greatly by artists of the Renaissance. Medalists such as Benvenuto Cellini and Antonio Pisanello used the obverse of the medal for the portrait and inscription of the person or event. The reverse of the medal referred to the symbolic meaning or significance of the person or event.
J.F.H.

109. *Carnegie Corporation Medal*, 1934
bronze
4½ x 4⅛
66.14.204
Murtha 335

The obverse of the medal depicts a scroll and a lighted lamp with the legend: *Presented by the Carnegie Corporation*. The reverse depicts Bellerophon, in his role as conquerer, taming the winged horse Pegasus with a golden bridle.
J.F.H.

110. *Maxfield Parrish Portrait Medal*, 1915
bronze
3¼ diameter
66.14.211
Murtha 65

Maxfield Parrish, an American artist known for illustrations and murals, also used mythological themes in his work. Parrish built a home in Cornish, New Hampshire; the "Cornish colony" popularized by Augustus Saint-Gaudens was a summer gathering place for artists. Manship spent the summers of 1915-1917 in Cornish and was Parrish's neighbor.

The obverse of the medal shows Parrish in profile. The reverse depicts the winged horse Pegasus. The reverse of the *Saint Paul Institute Medal*, 1916 (66.14.233) exhibits the same motif. Manship may have seen Cellini's similar imagery in his sixteenth century medals.
J.F.H.

111. *Defense of Verdun Medal*, 1921
bronze
4 diameter
66.14.219
Murtha 141

This medal was awarded for excellent
service in the American Marine Corps.
Manship did not always have the freedom
to choose the subjects for his medals, often
having to satisfy the requirements of a
commission. He took the same care,
however, in carving the medals and
medallions as in his other work, and was
especially concerned about the lettering.
The subject on the obverse of the medal
depicts an allegorical figure of France with
the inscription *To Commemorate the Defense of
Verdun 1916;* on the reverse, two soldiers
guard the gate of Verdun with the
inscription *Ils ne passeront pas.*
G.K.

112. *Kultur Medal*, 1918
bronze
5¼ diameter
66.14.238
Murtha 103

A controversial medal because of its
atypical subject matter, the obverse
portrays a thick-necked Kaiser with
horned helmet wearing a necklace of
skulls, bearing the inscription: *The Foe of
Free Peoples — His Rosary.* On the reverse is
a German soldier abducting a woman, her
child on the ground, with the inscription
"Kultur in Belgium — Murder Pillage,"
symbolizing the German blitzkrieg in
Belgium.
G.K.

113. *Study for Carnegie Corporation Medal*,
n.d.
ink and pencil on paper
4⅞ x 5¼
66.14.166f

This drawing was a study for the reverse of
the *Carnegie Corporation Medal* (109).
Manship made many subtle changes
between this drawing and the reverse of
the bronze medal. In the drawing of
Pegasus his mane is free flowing and he
wears no bridle. Bellerophon's right arm is
drawn back at shoulder level in the
drawing but held down against his body
and bent up and outward at the elbow in
the bronze sketch. The draperies of the
bronze version are more fluid in treatment,
giving the illusion of movement.
J.F.H.

114. *Roosevelt Inaugural Medal.* 1933
bronze
3 diameter
66.14.216
Murtha 332

Paul Manship was chosen by Robert W. Wooley, Chairman, Bureau of the Mint's Medals Committee, to design the Franklin Delano Roosevelt Inaugural Medal. Wooley, a friend of Roosevelt, described Manship in the following manner:

He has been long recognized as having few peers in this profession. Mr. Manship accepted the commission with enthusiasm, agreeing that his compensation should be relatively a nominal one. *

Manship also knew Roosevelt; in 1919 he had advised Roosevelt, then Assistant Secretary of the Navy, about a desired change in the design of the Navy's Medal of Honor. On the obverse, a portrait head of Roosevelt is depicted along with the following inscription: *Franklin Delano Roosevelt 31st President of the United States 1933-1937. John Nance Garner Vice President* The subject matter on the reverse was suggested by Roosevelt himself, acknowledging his past association with the Navy. Based on a 1789 print of the U.S. "Constitution," or "Old Ironsides," owned by Roosevelt, Manship designed a ship, beneath which is a winged woman symbolizing the "Ship of State." ** The inscription along the rim is a quotation from Longfellow:

Thou, too, sail on, O Ship of State, sail on, O union strong and great.

Manship also sculpted a *Franklin D. Roosevelt Memorial* in 1945. It is described by Murtha as a bronze tablet with a high

relief portrait. Its location, in 1957, was in Philadelphia, Reform Congregation, Kenesseth Israel.
*Neil MacNeil, *The President's Medal 1787-1977* (New York, 1977), 89.
**McNeil, 90
S.L.

Selected Bibliography

BOOKS AND EXHIBITION CATALOGUES

Agard, Walter Raymond. *Classical Myths in Sculpture*. Madison, Wis.: University of Wisconsin Press, 1951.

The Paul Manship Papers. Archives of American Art.
N 714 Personal calendars 1925-35, and 1937-61.
N 715 Personal calendars 1937-61, cont.
N 716 Personal calendars 1937-61, cont.
N 717 Personal calendars 1963-65.
N 62 Paul Manship scrapbooks.
NY 59-15 Paul Manship photographs, exhibition catalogues, clippings, writings, lectures, articles on sculpture, etc.
NY 59-16 Writings on art, family records, and correspondence 1933-57. Also correspondence A through N, dating 1940-47.
NY 59-17 Correspondence O through Z, 1940-47.

Averell House. *Sculpture by Paul Manship.* New York: 1933.

Berlin Photographic Company. *Catalogue of Sculpture by Paul Manship.* Introduction by Martin Birnbaum. New York: 1916.

Birnbaum, Martin. *Introductions.* New York: Frederic Fairchild Sherman, 1919.

Brookgreen Gardens, Brookgreen, S.C. *Sculpture by Paul Manship.* New York: 1938.

Casson, Stanley. *Twentieth Century Sculptors.* London: Oxford University Press, 1930.

A Century of American Sculpture, Treasures from Brookgreen Gardens. Introduction by A. Hyatt Mayor. New York: Abbeville Press, 1981.

Coen, Rena Neumann. *Painting and Sculpture in Minnesota 1820-1914.* Minneapolis: University of Minnesota Press, 1976.

Cortissoz, Royal. *American Artists.* New York: Charles Scribner's Sons, 1923.

Craven, Wayne. *Sculpture in America.* Newark, Delaware: University of Delaware Press, 1984.

Designs in Glass by 27 Contemporary Artists. New York: Steuben Glass, 1940.

Durman, Donald Charles. *He Belongs to the Ages. The Statues of Abraham Lincoln.* Ann Arbor, Mich.: Edwards Brothers, 1951.

Eisler, Colin. *Sculptors' Drawings Over Six Centuries 1400-1950.* New York: Agrinde Publications, 1981.

Failing, Patricia. *Best-Loved Art From American Museums.* An Artnews Book. New York: Clarkson N. Potter, 1983.

Fairmount Park Art Association, Philadelphia. *Sculpture of a City: Philadelphia's Treasures in Bronze and Stone.* New York: Walker Publishing, 1974.

Gallatin, Albert Eugene. *Paul Manship: A Critical Essay on his Sculpture, and an Iconography.* New York: John Lane, 1917.

Gardner, Albert T.E. *American Sculpture, A Catalogue of the Collections of The Metropolitan Museum of Art.* New York: Metropolitan Museum of Art, 1965.

Goode, James M. *The Outdoor Sculpture of Washington, D.C.* Washington, D.C.: Smithsonian Institution Press, 1974.

The Index of Twentieth Century Artists. John Shapley, ed. vol. 1 (November-December 1933): 30-36. vol. 2 suppl. (September 1935): 41. vol. 3 (August-September 1936): 40.

Isabella Stewart Gardner Museum. *Sculpture in the Isabella Stewart Gardner Museum.* Boston: 1977.

Lynch, Kenneth. *Sundials and Spheres.* The Architectural Handbook Series. Canterbury, Conn.: Canterbury Publishing, 1971.

MacNeil, Neil. *President's Medal 1789-1977.* Introduction by Marvin Sadik. Washington, D.C.: Smithsonian Institution, National Portrait Gallery, 1977.

McRoberts, Jerry William. *The Conservative Realists' Image of America in the 1920s: Modernism, Traditionalism and Nationalism.* Ann Arbor, Mich.: University Microfilms, 1980.

Mead, Franklin B. *Heroic Statues in Bronze of Abraham Lincoln, Introducing the Hoosier Youth of Paul Manship.* Fort Wayne, Ind.: Lincoln National Life Insurance Company, 1932.

Michigan State Library. *Biographical Sketches of American Artists.* 5th ed. Lansing, Mich.: 1924.

Miller, Alec. *Tradition in Sculpture.* New York and London: Studio Publications, 1949.

Minnesota Museum of Art. *Paul Howard Manship, An Intimate View: Sculpture and Drawings from the Permanent Collection of the Minnesota Museum of Art.* Saint Paul: 1972.

Murtha, Edwin. *Paul Manship.* New York: Macmillan, 1957.

The National Arts Club. *Paul Manship Memorial Exhibition.* New York: 1966.

National Sculpture Society. *Contemporary American Sculpture.* San Francisco: The California Palace of the Legion of Honor, 1929.

National Sculpture Society. *Exhibition of American Sculpture Catalogue.* New York: 1923.

National Sculpture Society. *Paul Manship.* New York: W.W. Norton and Company, 1947.

Norton Gallery of Art. *Catalogue of the Collection, Norton Gallery of Art.* West Palm Beach, Fla.: 1979.

Proske, Beatrice. *Brookgreen Gardens, Sculpture.* Brookgreen, S.C.: Brookgreen Gardens, 1943 and 1968.

The Saint Paul Art Center. *Spindrift.* vol. 2, no. 1. Saint Paul, Minn.: 1967.

Schnier, Jacques. *Sculpture in Modern America.* Berkeley and Los Angeles: University of California Press, 1948.

Smithsonian Institution. *A Retrospective Exhibition of Sculpture by Paul Manship.* Washington, D.C.: 1958.

Smithsonian Institution, National Collection of Fine Arts and the Saint Paul Art Center. *Paul Manship, 1885-1966.* Washington, D.C.: 1966.

Squire, C.B. *Outdoor Sculpture by Paul Manship.* Wilton, Conn.: Kenneth Lynch and Sons: n.d.

Vermeule, Cornelius. *Numismatic Art in America.* Cambridge, Mass.: Belknap Press of Harvard University, 1971.

Vitry, Paul. *Paul Manship, Sculpteur Americain.* Paris: Éditions de la Gazette des Beaux-Arts, 1927.

Walker Art Center. *Twentieth Century Sculpture: Selections from the Permanent Collection.* Minneapolis, Minn.: 1969.

Whitney Museum of American Art. *Two Hundred Years of American Sculpture.* New York: 1976.

ARTICLES

Adams, Herbert. "Paul H. Manship." *Art and Progress* 6 (November 1914): 20-24.

Beatty, Albert R. "Lincoln, the Youth in Bronze." *National Republic* (April 1933): 14-32.

Boutet de Monvel, Roger. "La Sculpture Decorative de Paul Manship." *Art et Industrie,* vol. 3, no. 12 (10 December, 1927): 33-37.

Breck, Joseph. "Playfulness." *Bulletin of The Minneapolis Institute of Arts* 3 (October 1914): cover, 125-126.

Cox, Kenyon. "A New Sculptor." *The Nation* 96 (13 February 1913): 162-163.

De Cisneros, Francois G. "La Maciza Escultura de Paul Manship." *Social* (October 1918): 16-18.

De Cuevas, George. "Paul Manship." *La Renaissance* 15 (July-September 1932): 131-135.

Ellis, F. L. "Manship's Freedom Stamp Design was Photo of a Plaster Cast." *Don Houseworth's International Stamp Review* 23 (April 1943): 1-3.

Ellis, Joseph Bailey. "Paul Manship in the Carnegie Institute." *The Carnegie Magazine* 2 (September 1937): 110-113.

"Exhibitions at the Art Institute; Sculpture by Paul Manship." *Fine Arts Journal* 33 (October 1915): 429-434.

Frost, R. "Manship Ahoy!" *Art News* 44 (June 1945): 28.

Gallatin, Albert Eugene. "An American Sculptor: Paul Manship." *The Studio* 82 (October 1921): 137-144.

———. "The Greatness of Paul Manship?" *Arts and Decoration* 6 (April 1916): 291, 294.

———. "The Sculpture of Paul Manship." *Bulletin of The Metropolitan Museum of Art* 11 (October 1916): 218-222.

Gallo-Ruiz, E. "Medal of Dionysus." *Numismatist* 57 (March 1944): 189-194.

Hancock, Walker. "Paul Manship." *Fenway Court,* Isabella Stewart Gardner Museum vol. 1, no. 1 (October 1966): 1-7.

Hind, C. Lewis. "Paul Manship." *The Saturday Review* 132 (2 July 1921): 10-11.

Humber, George. "Paul Manship." *The New Republic* 6 (25 March 1916): 207-209.

Kammerer, Herbert L. "In Memoriam — Paul Manship." *National Sculpture Review* vol. 14, no. 4 (Winter 1965-1966): 6-7.

———. "...Paul Manship, Fourteenth President, National Sculpture Society." *National Sculpture Review* vol. 15, no. 3 (Fall 1966): 22, 27-29.

"Lincoln Statue, Fort Wayne." *American Magazine of Art* 25 (September 1932): 182-183.

Maraini, Antonio. "Lo Scultore Paul Manship." *Dedalo* 4 (August 1923): 181-195.

McClinton, Katherine Morrison. "Paul Manship: American Sculptor." *Art and Antiques* vol. 5, no. 2 (March-April 1982): 94-99.

"A Modern Primitive in Art." *The Literary Digest* 52 (6 May 1916): 1278-1281.

"A New Sculptor." *The Outlook* 106 (14 February 1914): 335-337.

"Paul Manship — A Conversation." *Craft Horizons* vol. 2, no. 1 (November 1942): 7.

"Paul Manship, Sculptor." *Gopher Historian* (Winter 1967-1968): 1-8.

"Paul Manship's Dramatic Vision of John D. Rockefeller." *Current Opinion* 69 (July 1920): 96-98.

"Paul Manship's Work in Sculpture." *The Outlook* 112 (8 March 1916): 542-543, 553.

Payne, Frank Owen. "Two Amazing Portraits by Paul Manship." *International Studio* 71 (October 1920): 125-127.

Rather, Susan. "The Past Made Modern: Archaism in American Sculpture." *Arts Magazine* 59 (November 1984): 111-119.

Rogers, Cameron. "The Compleat Sculptor." *New Yorker Magazine* 4 (1 September 1928): 21-23.

Rubins, D.K. "Bronze by Paul Manship: Rape of Europa." *John Herron Art Institute Bulletin* 38 (April 1951): 1-3.

"A Tablet Erected by the Trustees of the Museum in Memory of the Late J. Pierpont Morgan." *Bulletin of The Metropolitan Museum of Art* 15 (1920): 265-267.

Van Rensselaer, Mariana Griswold. "Pauline." *Scribner's Magazine* 60 (December 1916): 772-776.

"Who is Who in Minnesota Art Annuals — Paul Manship." *The Minnesotan* vol. 1, no. 1 (July 1915): 14-17.

Wilson, Malin. "Paul Manship: *The Flight of Night.*" *Toledo Museum of Art, Museum News* vol. 17, no. 3 (1974): 59-61.

Index to Illustrations

Works not Illustrated

115. *Aquarius Ashtray*, 1946*
bronze
6″ diameter
Collection Mrs. Paul K. Manship

116. *Bellerophon and Pegasus*, 1958
bronze, marble base
7½ x 3½ x 3
National Museum of American Art,
Smithsonian Institution
Gift of the Estate of Paul Manship
1966.47.58

117. *Bulldog*, 1906
bronze
2⁵⁄₁₆ x 4¹⁄₁₆ x 1¹⁵⁄₁₆
National Museum of American Art,
Smithsonian Institution
Gift of the Estate of Paul Manship
1966.47.41

118. *Celestial Sphere*, 1934*
bronze, marble base
24 x 15 x 15
Collection American Museum—Hayden
Planetarium, New York

119. *Model for Centaurus*, 1934*
detail for 1939
Celestial Sphere
bronze
20½ x 32¼
Collection Mrs. Paul K. Manship

120. *The Country Mouse and the City Mouse*,
1952
bronze, marble base
7½ x 17¾ x 3⅝
National Museum of American Art,
Smithsonian Institution
Gift of the Estate of Paul Manship
1966.47.21

121. *Day and the Hours — Sundial*, 1916*
gilded bronze
1′8½″ x 1′6″
Anonymous loan

122. *Deer*, n.d.*
crayon on paper
5¾ x 11
Collection Bradley Bonse and Florence
Manship Bonse

123. *End of Day*, n.d.
terra cotta
9 x 12 x 7½
National Museum of American Art,
Smithsonian Institution
Gift of Paul Manship
1965.16.51

124. *Frog*, 1952
bronze, lapis lazuli base
2½ high
National Museum of American Art,
Smithsonian Institution
Gift of the Estate of Paul Manship
1966.47.31

125. *Greek Vase*, 1912
pencil on paper
8½ x 6
National Museum of American Art,
Smithsonian Institution
Gift of the Estate of Paul Manship
1966.47.238

126. *Head of Child*, n.d. (relief)*
painted terra cotta
16½ x 13
Collection Mr. and Mrs. O. N. Klatt

127. *Hercules and the Nemean Lion* (#1), n.d.
gilded bronze, marble base
8³⁄₁₆ x 7¾ x 3½
National Museum of American Art,
Smithsonian Institution
Gift of the Estate of Paul Manship
1966.47.68

128. *Details from Stained Glass Window,
Poitiers*, 1922
pencil on paper
14¹⁄₁₆ x 9¹¹⁄₁₆
National Museum of American Art,
Smithsonian Institution
Gift of the Estate of Paul Manship
1966.47.213

*Saint Paul showing only

Board of Trustees

Staff

DIRECTOR'S OFFICE

M.J. Czarniecki III, *Director*
Joanna Baymiller, *Deputy Director*
Janet P. Bisbee, *Development Specialist*
Timothy Jennen, *Assistant to the Director*

PRIMARY PROGRAMS

Collections
Gloria Kittleson, *Curator of Collections*
Leanne Klein, *Associate Curator for
Collections Management*
Jean F. Hunter, *Assistant Curator for
Research*
Mary Holbrook, *Curatorial Assistant*

Education
Marcia Soderman-Olson, *Associate Curator
of Education*
Mary Altman, *Assistant Curator of
Education*
Karen Mueller, *Assistant Curator of
Education*
Holly Wolhart, *Education Assistant*

Exhibitions
James D. Ristine, *Curator of Exhibitions*
Katherine Van Tassell, *Assistant Curator for
Registration*
David Madzo, *Curatorial Assistant*
Stafford Taylor, *Curatorial Assistant*
Timothy White, *Curatorial Assistant*
Julia Schreifels, *Design Technician*

SUPPORT PROGRAMS

James J. Kamm, *Assistant Director*
Ramona Frana, *Support Programs Assistant*

Marketing
Nell McClure, *Marketing Supervisor*
Julia Schreifels, *Graphics Specialist*

Media Relations
Patricia Heikenen, *Media Relations
Supervisor*
Marjorie Casey, *Media Relations Specialist*

Membership
Sayre Carlson, *Membership Specialist*
Ramona Frana, *Membership Assistant*

Personnel
Jean F. Hunter, *Personnel Supervisor*
Nell McClure, *Volunteer Supervisor*

Physical Plant
Terry Hildebrand, *Physical Plant Supervisor*
Daniel Fischback, *Physical Plant Technician*

Safety and Security
Thomas Stanger, *Specialist*
David Koepke, *Officer*
Michael Rabe, *Officer*
Cathy Adams, *Officer*
Anna Antoniou, *Officer*
Herbert Bausch, *Officer*
John Diebel, *Officer*
Laura Manske, *Officer*
Dierdre McClure, *Officer*
Hieu Nguyen, *Officer*
James Peterson, *Officer*
Rachel Zemmer, *Officer*

FINANCE/ENTERPRISE
PROGRAMS

Paul R. Orman, *Assistant Director*
Linda Larson, *Finance Assistant*
Patricia Heikenen, *Excursions Specialist*
Kay Eckstein, *Purchasing Technician*
Karen Kapphahn, *Accounting Technician*

Photography Credits

All photography is by Shin Koyama, Minneapolis, with the exception of the following individuals and institutions whose generosity is gratefully acknowledged: Alinari-Art Resource, NY: Fig. 7; American Academy in Rome, NY: Fig. 14; The Art Institute of Chicago: 94; Badisches Landesmuseum, Karlsruhe, W. Germany: Fig. 15; Solon Borglum Sculpture Project: 8; Breger & Associates; courtesy Corcoran Gallery of Art: 41; Geoffrey Clements, courtesy Century Association, NY: Fig. 27; City of New York, Parks & Recreation, Photographic Archive: Fig. 13; Cowan Pottery Museum, Rocky River, OH: 16; Deutsches Archaologisches Institut, Athens: Fig. 9; eeva-inkeri: 3; Peter A. Juley and Son Collection, National Museum of American Art, Smithsonian Institution, J0039148: Fig. 1, J0085221: Fig. 24, J0085229: Fig. 25, J0085187: Fig. 26, J0085232: Fig. 28; Mr. and Mrs. O.N. Klatt: Fig. 2; Mr. and Mrs. John Manship: Fig. 4, 5, 12; 106, 107; Mrs. Paul K. Manship: Fig. 22; Marion Koogler McNay Art Institute, San Antonio: 67; Jerry Mathiason: 100; William Meng, courtesy New York Zoological Society: Fig. 11; The Metropolitan Museum of Art: Fig. 3; The Minneapolis Institute of Arts: 48; Montclair Art Museum: 7; National Museum of American Art, Smithsonian Institution: 1, 10, 13, 15, 25, 32, 40, 70, 72, 73, 83, 87, 97, 98; New York Public Library: Fig. 10; Susan Rather: Fig. 6, 8; Rockefeller Foundation: Fig. 16; William Ryan, courtesy 3M: Fig. 29, 30; Saint Paul Pioneer Press Dispatch, courtesy Minnesota Historical Society: Fig. 23; Mr. and Mrs. Gerald Peters: 99; Smith College Museum of Art: 42; United Nations, Geneva, Switzerland: Fig. 20; Peter M. Warner, Nyack, NY: Fig. 17, 18, 19, 21.

Colophon

This catalogue was printed in an edition of 2500 by West Publishing Company and was bound by Midwest Editions. The color separations were made by Colorhouse, Inc. The type is Garamond and was set by Alphagraphics One on a Mergenthaler 202. The catalogue was designed by Kathe Wilcoxon.